alone & together

the writers collective

poetry & prose

Curated by
MaryAnn Easley, Kimberly Krantz & Sheila Roell

Windflower Press
A Boutique Publisher
Orange County, California

A Boutique Publisher
Orange County, California

Alone & Yet Together

The Writers Collective

Curated & edited by: MaryAnn Easley, Kimberly Krantz & Sheila Roell

Published in the United States of America

Windflower Press, Laguna Niguel, CA 92607, 949-285-3831

Books in Print.

ISBN: 9798396277571

Printed in the United States of America on acid-free paper.

First Edition.

Paperback.

Cover/book design: Jann Harmon - 949-291-3977

Alone & Yet Together, The Writers Collective: anthology, collection, poetry, haiku, rondelet, free verse, fiction, memoir, drabbles, essays, satire, humor.

Dedication

This book is dedicated to the mentors and coaches who inspire writers to believe in themselves and trust their instincts, spark creativity in the writing process, and offer critique to bring out the best in each writer.

And to our writing communities, where we engage, support, and nurture each other. This allows writers to mentor, and mentors to write. Through this process, we gain the assurance to write alone and yet together.

Contents

Introduction

As writers, we scribble our thoughts in solitude, often late at night when the moon is full or while noticing an altered slant of light through a café window. We delve into our creative souls alone to find the rough clay needed for our art. We do this through journaling and self-reflection.

Eventually, however, we emerge from our seclusion to find others who share the same obsession with writing and the same journey. It's within this circle of like-minded individuals that we discover the opportunity to reach our full potential. This writing community offers solace and is the place where we find new perspectives about our work-in-progress.

Writers investing in other writers also invest in themselves. Carl Sagan said that writing is perhaps the greatest of human inventions, binding together people and citizens of distant epochs who never knew one another. "Books break the shackles of time—proof that humans can work magic."

While writing can be a lonely endeavor, we've learned that we're each talented in different ways, and these talents are gifts we can share to create magic. Whether our purpose for writing is for self-expression, healing, communication with others, or writing a best seller, we find the courage and confidence to claim ourselves as writers while receiving wisdom from others. As we give and receive, we become part of a greater whole, expressing ourselves via the creative force that moves through us all.

This collection of poetry, fiction, and memoir is a celebration of a network of individuals who write alone and yet bravely join a community where their art is better manifested. It has been our honor to recognize and support this collective of talented individuals.

"We do not live or create in isolation. Each of us is part of a greater whole and, as we agree to express ourselves, we agree to express the larger Self that moves through us all."

— Julia Cameron, *Walking in this World*

A Writer

by Nancy Pfaffl

I am a writer.
Writing is my art.
My art may be different than your art.
Both are unique and to be shared.

I am a poet.
My poetry is my experience.
My experience may differ from yours.
Yet all have value.

I am a writer and a poet.
Writing and poetry are from my perspective.
My perspective on the world may be different
    from your perspective
Equally important.

I am a writer and a poet.
My writing and poetry are unique to me.
When we share our words
We share our reality, perspective, experiences.

I am a writer.
Language is the artist's brush of my life.
When I share my words
I speak my truth.

The Tiny Red Stapler

by JG McCrillis

A student shambles past the attractive slim figured young blonde waiting at the door. He turns and looks back, mouth gaping, eyes shocked, head hanging, shoulders stooped. He turns again and slinks out the Registrar office disappearing into the shadows.

#64 flashes on the queue sign. The girl's number. She strides into the office, her blonde ponytail bouncing back and forth. She makes her way to the desk at the far end of the room, the same one vacated by the boy who passed her in the doorway.

The man at the desk sits facing away from her as she approaches. She slides into the chair on the opposite side and flashes a bright smile. The man owns a three-day stubble, bagged eyes and a pallor suggestive of a hangover. He glances at her dismissively, looks off to the side, shuts his eyes. Her smile weakens a bit. He gives her a bored nod and gestures with his fingers for her to speak.

"Hi…ah…I'd like to register for my classes." She says it with a lilt, like a question…*my classes?*

He gives her an aloof cursory look. Taking his time, he reaches for a thermos on the desk. "Just a second." He slowly pours coffee into a paper cup, lifts it to his lips, then slides open a drawer in his desk, takes out a toothpick, puts it in his mouth.

As she watches and waits, her smile fades. A hint of unease spreads over her face; her shoulders go a little slack.

Without making eye contact, he says, "Information desk," he cocks his head toward the door, "Form A2176. Fill it out and—"

Before he can finish, she reaches into her bag and

extracts Form A2176 and places it on the desk before him. "Already filled it out." Her smile returns, her posture perks up.

He leans back in his swivel chair, looks up at her with hooded eyes, slides the form toward him, glances at it, then pushes it away, gives a rueful smile and says, "You haven't marked this box." He taps a small box on the form in the lower left corner. "Go back to the desk at the entrance and—"

She whips out two more sheets, and this time, slaps them down. "I made out two other copies—revised." She pushes them across the desk.

The dozen or so other office clerks have taken notice of a rising tension in the room. Goggling at what they see, as if with hushed dread, they've grown still sensing the man's rising hackles. His face flushes. He glares at one of the gawking workers who quickly looks away and resumes typing on his computer.

The girl is now staring bayonets at him.

He picks up the other two forms, chews his toothpick, collects all three pages, taps the edges together, lays them down, slides them back toward her, takes the toothpick from his mouth, rolls it in his fingers for a moment, puts it back in his mouth. Without looking at her, "You're missing your financial state—."

Keeping her narrowed eyes fixed on him, she smacks the completed statement on the desk before he can finish the word.

He's startled, but quickly bounces back with, "… and the copy."

She glowers at him as she draws the copy from her bag and slaps it on the desk along with the original.

He raises his chin, looks down at it, spits out his toothpick and glares back at her, "All right, Blondie, you asked for it." He rises out of his chair, leans on his fists, "Photocopy of I.D."

Slapped down.

"Photocopy of birth certif—."

Slapped down.

"Photocopy of Social Security Car…"

Smacked down.

"Photocopy of passport."

Slapped down.

"Driver's licen—"

Smacked down.

"Library car—"

Whipped out and thwacked on the desk. Seething, she glares at him.

He looks away, breathing with exasperation. Then comes back once more, "Double copy of Form 6971d."

Smiling with scorn, she pulls two sheets from her bag, brandishes them, one in each hand beside her ears. *Check.*

He adds, "Numbered and stapled."

Defiance falls from her face. *The stapled requirement.* She looks up at him.

He repeats with glee, "Stapled!" *Check. He's got her.*

Unnerved, she glances furtively around the office. He follows the path her eyes take as her scrutiny falls onto the next desk. There it is. A shiny metal stapler. Like a showdown at high noon, there's a pause. They both know what is about to happen. They both lunge for it. He beats her to the draw, steps back, holds it up gloating, taunting her. *Double check.*

Her mouth gapes open, her eyes widen. Then, slowly she extends her right arm and shaking her hand like Travis Bickle in *Taxi Driver*, slides from her sleeve…a tiny red stapler.

The workers gasp. Like helpless onlookers at a blood bath, some can't take their riveted stares off the horror playing out in front of them. Others hide their eyes.

The girl raises the little red stapler, clicks it twice. *Checkmate.*

His face goes slack. He drops the shiny metal stapler and crumbles back into his seat uttering, "No…no, not the tiny red stapler." Like he's bought a bullet, he topples forward. The side of his face falls flat onto his desk, his eyes—a wide vacant stare, his mouth agape.

She steps back to the desk, her lips pressed tight. She staples the two sheets together, flings them down before his vanquished eyes, takes his limp hand, places it on the metal stamper and with her hand pushes his hand down stamping all pages twice.

Straightening up, tall, proud and blonde, she gathers her bag and begins to march out the office. Like the Red Sea, the stunned workers part the way for her. The click of her heels on the floor, the only sound, as she strides past them. Her ponytail sways side to side.

My Infinity Pool

by Kimberly Krantz

I can sit – for hours
    within the confines of this body
        lost in thought and staring into space, or at my feet
            listing what keeps me awake, all the time
                not hearing the chaos around me
                    not seeing if anyone notices *me*

I can't stand up yet
    despite my intentions
        so many more 'what if's' to work through
            screaming on the outside to quiet the inside
                creating plans, back-up plans, back-up plans to the
            back-up plans
                    i have visions of going home to meet those
                    who went before *me*

It just never seems to end - -
        that infinity pool is always full - -
            and always calling *me*

blackberry picking

by Chris Perry

it's june, and hot, but not as hot
as the kitchen where she's baking
scones, so i wear my thornproof
barbour coat and some shorts,

stepping on the most brutal crazy vines,
leaning slowly, with patience,
my chest and belly at the skewers,
to reach with my long arm

into the gnarl, seeking the lusty clutch,
which has been kept safe from
birds and raccoons and humans
without strong coats and enough desire;

many crawl with ants but that,
and the ecstatic ease with which
they release and slush and bleed,
lets me know they are good.

we make savory whipped cream,
with a little salt instead of sugar,
and tear blenheim apricots to jam
with our fingers, and somehow

there are twelve or fifteen of us!
and even a dog! and i can't wait
to kiss you. later, we drive to the hill
and park precariously on a slope:

it is grey and the wind is flying.
we find a rock and sit close. some dogs
wonder at flying odors, and from our rock
on the hill, we can see another hill,

green with heavy trees, and close,
like everything here except the bridge,
so we wend our way down helpless
trails and it is suddenly as sunny

as a sunny day, and there is a flotilla
of tangles as big as a backyard,
mazy like on purpose; we penetrate
into the, my god, it feels like a temple,

and seek the last greatest ones of
july and sight again the other hill,
green, from our balcony of thorns.
and later, there are brambles but no berries,

and i am drunken and wild for her,
and we sneak into a backyard's bush
and i kiss her. my god!
if only everyplace could be one place!

"How vain it is to sit down to write when you have not stood up to live."

—Henry David Thoreau

Swept Away by the Tide

by Prem Saint

I usually love the ocean, but today I hate it as I swim across Tudor Bay in Mombasa to reach the mainland. A gust of wind stirs up a wave that washes over my face and the salt stings my eyes. I shut my burning eyes and swim hard towards the beach across the bay. When I pause to gauge where I'm heading, I realize that the sea is sucking me towards Nyali Bridge and the Indian Ocean where sharks abound. I'm not a strong swimmer, but I try anyway to battle the warm water using a breaststroke. To catch my breath and to rest my aching arms, I briefly float on my back and try to push away the voice that echoes a reprimand.

What a stupid idea to swim the channel on my last day in Mombasa.

It's the Second of September 1955. I have won a Kenya Government Scholarship to study in England. Tomorrow afternoon I am taking a train for Nairobi to catch a flight to London. I have been teaching at Mbheni Primary School, Mombasa for over two years. Ever since I left high school, with a Cambridge School Certificate and a London Matriculation, I have been obsessed with the idea of going to England. Not so much to learn there, but to come back to Kenya with the label of 'England Returned.' Then I will walk around with an air of sophistication, speaking *proper* English and eating with a fork and knife. And I might have a fling with ballroom dancing.

For the last few months, along with some friends, I have been riding my bike to the Tudor Beach to swim across to the mainland. This has been a welcome relief from the hectic preparations for traveling to England. Two years ago, my brother won a scholarship to study in England and has been writing about his adventures in Yorkshire and in Scotland, encouraging me to consider doing the same. His advice of volunteering for extracurricular activities in our school led to my becoming a Scout Master, Prefect Master, and winning awards in our school's Physical Education competitions. I must have impressed them sufficiently because I have been awarded the scholarship. Now I must get some warm clothing for England.

In the tropical climate of Mombasa, I do not need a jacket. In fact, in 1953, for my passport photo I had to borrow my father's jacket and ask him for help with the tie. Now I have my own jacket, and I am ready to go to England.

But today, instead of packing my suitcase, my friend, Yash, persuades me to swim the channel for old times' sake, so I took off to Tudor beach. We locked our bikes, selected the abandoned cottage on a beach across the bay for our target and jumped in.

Mombasa is an island connected to the mainland by Makupa Causeway to the north, Nyali Bridge to the east and Likoni Ferry to the south. Tudor Bay, also called Port Tudor, is located to the north of the Nyali Bridge. Yash and I live in the same Government Quarters and can reach the Tudor Beach on our bicycles within half-an-hour. Normally we would have our swim and return home before sunset before my father returns from the Railway Club. Today our swim is becoming crazy because of the strong ebb tide caused by the full moon.

When I find myself being sucked under by the sea, I panic.

"Help, Help!"

In the distance, I can hear Yash calling for help as well. I pray that a boat will somehow appear and rescue us.

"Help, Help!"

My shouts are interrupted by saltwater filling my mouth. From the corner of my eye, I see the moon rising and pray to *Varuna,* the Hindu Ocean Deity, for help, as I keep swimming and shouting for help.

Then I see a motorboat approaching.

"Need a ride?" someone shouts. A European gentleman appears to be piloting the boat.

"Yes. Yes, please."

He helps me climb into the boat and I slump onto the seat. I mutter something about my friend and soon we hear his yells of "Help, Help."

Together we pull Yash on board.

When we are deposited on Tudor Beach, we profusely thank the gentleman and again collapse on the warm sand. After we gather enough strength, we ride our bikes home by the light of the full moon.

Fortunately, my father has not returned from the club. I hurriedly eat dinner brought in by our houseboy-cook and start packing my suitcase. I go to bed exhausted, but filled with gratitude for the European gentleman, for the deity *Varuna*, and for the Kenya Government for the scholarship to study in England.

The next day I do not tell my father about the incident for fear of being reprimanded.

Later my father and several friends, including Yash, come to Mombasa railway station to see me off. Yash comes into my compartment and shows me a clipping from "Mombasa Times" which describes how Dr. Keatings saved two Indian boys from drowning. I give him a smile and we say goodbye.

As soon as I settle down in my seat, the train starts to move. I shut my eyes and reflect upon the recent tide episode. Suddenly, several events come to mind. I realize that I'd been swept away by the tide of history, from Pakistan to India, and then from India to Kenya. Going to England with a scholarship on my own initiative, is the first time when I am actually riding the wave of controlling my own destiny. I decide I must make more conscientious decisions when I'm in England.

Recalling these events after 66 years, I am gratified to have built confidence in riding the wave of destiny, finishing my university degrees, and making the decision to move from Kenya to America. Now I notice my children and grandchildren riding the waves of their academic and professional lives. That includes our grandson, Ashton, a true Southern California boy and a surfer. Ashton can vouch for the thrill of riding the *real* ocean waves.

Aging
by MJ West

After months of waiting
for her arrival,
I finally meet her face to face and
caress her fresh, cherub skin.

Gazing at a photo of me
cradling
my first great-grandchild,

I hardly recognize myself,
I look so different,

and yet…
I feel the same inside.

How did life go by so quickly?

Tenderness of many images
have stayed with me and
will never be lost
or forgotten.

There are no wrinkles
in my mind or
in my spirit.

Love is a Rondelet

by MaryAnn Easley

You met me there
in the new writing class that night.
You met me there
disguised behind a brooding glare.
So brokenhearted was the sight,
I vowed to change your dark to light.
You met me there.

You promised me
the sea, the stars, the sky, the clouds.
You promised me
a life beyond the bourgeoisie,
refuge from the incessant crowds,
grace in lightness the moon enshrouds.
You promised me.

Grateful am I
for Choice, the dream where we belong.
Grateful am I
for evening sea and morning sky.
I knew I loved you all along
when you were you, and you were strong.
Grateful am I.

Much wiser now
seasoned by stark reality.
Much wiser now.
Love's hard but loving anyhow.
Nothing in life is granted free,
the steep price is mortality.
Much wiser now.

This much is true:
love will change your life forever.
This much is true:
be cautious if his eyes are blue.
Though love is a fine endeavor,
you are changed, but love changes too.
This much is true.

The Dressing Room Dilemma

by Angela Tippell

I had purchased an Italian knit dress, very lovely, but somewhat unforgiving of any bulge, bra, or panty line. So, a suitable undergarment was required. This was BS – Before Spanx. I went to Macy's lingerie department and perused the rails of full-length slips until I found some elasticated styles. Locating one wired at the bust, eliminating the need to wear a bra, I took my size and headed to the dressing rooms.

I stripped down to my panties and panty hose and started to put the slip on over my head. The elastic was somewhat tight; that would be good under the knit dress. Not so good struggling to get into it. I had my left arm through the strap and my left breast somewhat secured into the wired area that formed a bra. The rest of the garment was slung around my neck, my right arm nowhere near the strap, which seemed to be bunched up somewhere. My right breast hung pressed beneath the bunched up tight fabric. I could not stand up straight. My hose started to slip, taking my panties with them. Baggy crotch feeling, along with that of great discomfort and insecurity.

Then, the sudden realization that there may be a security camera in the dressing room flipped me into a panic. In my restricted bent-over position, I started to slowly circle the dressing room with my head cocked to one side, eyes darting maniacally. I must have resembled Quasimodo's twin sister. I imagined two security guards sitting in a room at the back of the store, their bank of TVs monitoring the dressing rooms. Probably a fat middle-aged man with his uniform stretched over his fat gut. Sitting there eating snacks, chomping, and nodding as he watched the screen, cracker crumbs falling into his Tom Selleck-style moustache. Next to him would be a skinny young man in a uniform a bit too large, with acne and greasy hair, staring at the screen and twitching.

I realized by now that I should have stepped into the garment. Too late to wiggle it down. I anchored myself against the wall for leverage with my right arm flaying around, finally working the *Iron Maiden* torture garment over my head and off. In the process, bringing down my up-do hairstyle and knocking off the small diamond earring that I had in the second piercing in my lobe. Not a large diamond by any means, but a diamond nonetheless. On my hands and knees to search for it, I crept around the dressing room floor in only my panties and pantyhose.

Having finally located the earring, I flung on my clothes, straightened my hair, and glanced around the dressing room to see if there were security cameras. There were none readily visible to a would-be shoplifter. I then exited the dressing room with as much dignity as I could muster, just in case there were cameras, took the garment to the sales counter, paid, and beat a hasty retreat from the store.

"Take off your armor; dare to be vulnerable, dare to unwrap yourself, and dare yourself to be yourself."

—*Maria Shriver*

Street Dance
by Sheila Roell

I was in Morocco the other day
Marrakesh, to be precise.
While on the medina
I spied
a dervish whirling my way.

All bounce and energy,
he gave the briefest glance,
to my pocketed hand.
Spinning round and round
he took a second look.

Then, with a nod from me
the street dance began.
He jumped, danced, bounced
up, down and all around,
a mix of color and sound.

With one arm pointed skyward, and
one, more earthbound, he soared
as the cymbals chimed on ankles, wrists,
and fingers, nimble enough
to make a joyful sound.

Dressed in red and gold
with tassels on his purple hat.
wearing a fingerless glove
to cover his ancient hand.
The dervish dipped, dashed,

and danced my way.
Catching his eye, I jingled my coins,
as he spun away.
In a swirl of color
His tassels awhirl.

A crowd gathered
vying for him,
but he whirled and swirled,
earning
what I kept hid

Oh, I thought
Is he dancing for one,
for all or just me?
He whirled close and winked.
'for the pretty lady,' he vowed

with a nod and smile,
allowing the sun
to glisten off a golden tooth.
Away he went
playing a kazoo, he produced.

Finally, I nodded, and he skipped near
on jeweled, purple,
slippered feet.
I laughed, and, smiled, and
stretched out my clenched fist.

With a glance at me
he reached his leathery hand
to mine.
My fingers uncurled
so he could see.

Upon my nod,
like a bird, he plucked
one coin per time
one, two, three coins or more
From my soft palm to his leathered one.

A happy, whirling street dancer
Swirled, dipped, and winked
paused a moment longer
and with a bow
melted merrily away.

Yes, I was in Morocco
the other day
Marrakesh, to be precise
By chance I met a dervish
And this magical memory came my way.

"We write to taste life twice, in the moment and in retrospect."

— *Anaïs Nin*

(Untitled)

by Momoyo Capanna

morning mist
yellow-orange Iceland poppies
bloom on his birthday

Find A Garden

by Jennifer Black, MD

I was in the operating room when the surgeons found
Mr. A's tumor. It had blocked off his stomach, spread up to
his liver, and crept across his abdomen to the pancreas. It
felt, as cancer does, like concrete within soft, warm putty.
The surgeons shook their heads; since the cancer had
spread, it could not be removed, so there seemed to be
nothing more they could do. They put in a feeding tube so
he could receive liquid artificial nutrition through the small
intestine. I was the new medical student, and new medical
students just follow orders, so when ordered, I stapled the
skin closed.

It was my first clinical rotation, and he was my first
patient. A surgery 'rotation'—a month-long assignment for a
doctor in training—means arriving at 5 AM daily to assemble
lab tests, x-rays, and patient vitals. It means working long days
and, often, long nights too. It meant being sleep-deprived,
on edge, and always prepared to answer tough questions
about your patient's illnesses. This patient, Mr. A, was
previously healthy and only 53 years old. He was admitted
to the hospital for dehydration due to non-stop vomiting. It
started months earlier when he noticed stomach pain when
eating. When it didn't resolve, he saw his doctor, who gave
him an antacid medication. When this didn't help, the doc
prescribed a more potent acid blocker. During that same
year, Mr. A's 20-year-old son had died in a car accident; so,
when the pain worsened and Mr. A began to feel full after
small meals, the doctor blamed stress and anxiety related
to this tragic loss. When Mr. A lost 50 pounds in just a few
months, the physician attributed it to depression. So, no tests
were done. Finally, when Mr. A couldn't hold down even sips

of water, he was sent to our large county hospital. Testing was finally done, and my team took him in for surgery.

Later, on rounds—a time when medical teams in training hospitals walk together to see their patients—Mr. A was told we had found cancer. Details of the procedure were described, but after he heard the "c-word," I don't think he could have taken in much more. And like many of our patients at County, English was not Mr. A's first language. The conversation was brief, and the team rushed off to see the next patient.

The following day, when I made rounds with the surgery chief, we visited Mr. A. The surgery chief mentioned, almost in passing ...the cancer in your abdomen..." Mr. A bolted upright and stared at me, wide-eyed: "You mean I still have cancer?" By then, surgery rounds being what they are, the chief had left me and moved on to the next patient. I stayed behind and explained to Mr. A what we'd seen in the OR, and what this meant. I walked with him for a while, pushing his IV pole. He cried and shared his fears. He showed me pictures of his newborn grandson in Hawaii, whom he feared he might never meet. And finally, he expressed sadness that his primary care physician had not heard him when he related his worsening symptoms. When the chief called from another patient's room to look for me, I explained that Mr. A had questions and asked if he had told him anything more about his cancer. "Yes, but he just didn't understand. So where are you, anyway? You need to get to the 10th floor now!"

Mr. A remained in the hospital for a while, while our team started tube feedings and prepared him for discharge. He was told that "nothing could be done." Each day, I stopped to spend a few minutes with Mr. A. One evening, he insisted we take a walk outside. "I want to show you something," he said excitedly. Outside our plain urban county facility in the middle of a less-than-attractive part of town, he'd found a garden. It was small but beautiful—a bright green, blue, and red speck in a grey downtown landscape. I'd never noticed it, though I'd walked past it daily for several weeks. I sat down. I touched a small flower growing up through a crack in the concrete. I smelled the grass, recently mowed, warmed by the sun. "La vida se abre paso," he said. Life finds a way.

Mr. A was discharged soon after our walk. He left town to be with his family. I never saw him again. That month, I learned a lot about wound care, surgical technique, postoperative fever, ventilator management, and other topics crucial to the care of a surgical patient. But Mr. A was the first of many patients who taught me invaluable lessons I didn't learn from my formal training—concepts I didn't fully appreciate until years later when I became a primary care and hospice physician:

Listen to your patients. Think twice before dismissing a complaint as "just stress."

Sit down. Explain things clearly, in words your patient can understand.

Check in to see what they're thinking and feeling. Offer empathy. Give comfort. You can always do something even when you can't cure the illness.

Find your own 'garden': take off the time you have earned. Do things that make life meaningful and fun, even if you're a busy doctor, a harried medical student, an overwhelmed teacher, or a stressed-out mom. Even if (well, even *when*---) you're dying.

Thank you for the lessons, Mr. A.

"No tears in the writer, no tears in the reader. No surprise in the writer, no surprise in the reader."

—*Robert Frost*

Vision

by J. Hanson

A vision
A reality
A fantasy made
A hope
A loving dedication
Designed by need, feeling, and imagination
An image on a screen, an image through
thought. A picture made of dreams
and manifested,
sought.

Time

by Nicole Sandoval Gurgone

I wear this weathered watch
Not to tell time
To remember times
Feels like yesterday
Like no time has passed
Time borrowed
Buried feelings
Deep down within
Lessons learned
Loved shared
Looking at your watch
Reminds me
Just how much you really cared

"Let me live, love, and say it well in good sentences."
— Sylvia Plath, The Unabridged Journals of Sylvia Plath

A Wedding Story
by Karen Ward

Three days before the wedding, I sat on the green sofa across from my father in the small living room of my parents' Victorian house on Cape Cod. It had been their home since they had retired three years earlier, moving from our family home in Wakefield, Massachusetts. At 68, my father's irreverent sense of humor was still much in evidence, as was his over-the-top pride in me. He approved of my upcoming marriage to David.

"First time she ever brought home a normal one!" he had said upon their meeting.

Bare trees outside the front window let in the low winter light as we chatted. I was filling him in on the last-minute details. David's mother had made all the arrangements for a rehearsal dinner at Anthony's Pier 4 in Barnstable. The menu and music for the reception were all set. The table candles would now be white, not red, the only change I had made to my mother's extensive planning for the Christmastime event to be held at the rambling Country Inn in Harwichport.

The marriage would take place at my parents' church, St. Pious X, a modern structure just a mile down the road from their South Yarmouth home. David and I had planned the ceremony, which involved a delicate balancing of required Catholic Church elements, deference to David's Protestant family, and accommodating our thoughts about marriage and life. Just months out of law school, we— well, I guess, mostly I—had some strong opinions about equality, independence, and being married. I would keep my birth—not maiden!—name. That battle with David's mom had been won after I proposed an alternative—just living together instead of getting married; she abruptly backed down. And we—well, mostly I—were writing our own vows, complete with footnotes acknowledging Shakespeare's contribution and promises not only of mutual love but mutual—and equal—well . . . everything.

Now we were talking about logistics. I was filling my dad in on how the processions would go—bride, bridesmaids, groomsmen, ushers, etc. A feminist, I chafed at the idea of being "given away" by one man to another. So I explained to my dad that I would be walking down the aisle alone, and he would walk with my mother.

At that, I saw his face fall. He was silent for a beat or two. Then he said, in almost a whisper, "Why aren't . . . you . . . doing it . . . the regular way?"

I thought my heart would break.

Not responding, I quickly went on to talk about other details, and we wrapped up the wedding discussions for the day.

As casually as I could the next morning, I explained to the assembled family how things would work. Completely ignoring the earlier discussion, I explained that I would walk down the aisle with Dad, and David would walk with his mother. That's the way I wanted it, and that's the way it would be.

The chaos and missteps of last-minute wedding preparation and festivities consumed the remaining days before the wedding, which was to commence at 3 p.m. on December 29, 1973.

On that day, a few minutes before three, my father, William J. Ward, Jr., appeared at the church wearing a topcoat and tails—the first in his life—and sporting a white carnation. His carefully combed full head of white hair fell gently against the stiff collar of his shirt, and his weathered, handsome face beamed. A broad smile spread across his face as I greeted him.

When the organist commenced The Wedding March, I took his arm. And, then, my father walked his cherished feminist-lawyer-daughter down the aisle to meet her bridegroom.

I later learned that weeks before, he had said of my wedding day,

"It's the last day I'll be important."

The Old Man and the Boy

by John Perry

An old man once strolled
Where the breakers rolled
Down by a wintry sea
A young man at his side
Matching stride on stride
Talking of times that used to be.

About days full of sun
When they would run
Down to the warmth of the sand
Where wonderful talks
Accompanied long walks
With small fingers in a gnarled old hand.

What stories he'd tell
Of ships under sail
When he worked each day on the docks
He told of his life
The sea and his wife
And the first time they'd come to these rocks

He spoke of past days
When the sea filled his gaze
Now his eyes beheld no joy
Once beautiful scenes
Lived only in dreams
Seen through the eyes of the boy

With unsteady gait
Though his path followed straight
On through the twilight he pressed
His pace never slowed
'Til his worn boot toed
The place on the shore he loved best

They spent this cold day
'Til the sun went away
Though the chill cut through to the bone
And he stayed to the end
With his Grandpa and friend
And the old man died not alone.

What to Eat

by Jim Black

"Are you hungry?"

"Yes!" I texted back.

"Great, I'm in the car. Let's go!"

I grabbed a sweatshirt and flip-flops and headed for the door. Lisa was waiting in the driveway, and I hopped in the passenger side.

"Do you want to drive?" she asked.

Uh oh. I knew trouble was on its way. Whoever drives usually has to decide where to go.

This was your idea, I thought to myself, *please don't tell me you don't have a plan!* "Uh, sure," I said, and we both exited and circled around the car. Once I was behind the wheel, I took the offensive. "Where shall we go?" I asked.

"Oh, wherever is fine with me."

I rolled my eyes and backed out of the driveway. The old *I'm agreeable to whatever you choose* trick. It makes the appearance of being magnanimous while actually creating a burden for the other person! Very sneaky.

In a country where food is so abundant, we sure have a hard time figuring out where to feed ourselves. We have too many options and not enough choices all at the same time.

I headed toward town, running the list of restaurants through my head.

Too fancy.

Too long of a wait.

We just ate there two days ago.

Too fattening.

Too casual (as if that's even possible).

"How about Another Kind Cafe?" she asked.

"That's too far!" I protested as if she suggested we

embark on a lengthy road trip instead of a 20-minute drive across town. "I'm hungry now. I can't wait that long."

"Ok fine." She sounded annoyed.

We drove along the PCH, passing mom and pop joints. Colombian. Mexican. Burgers. Bar food.

"Let's get pizza," I said, finally.

"No, I don't want pizza."

I waited. Nothing followed.

"Ok, then what?"

"I don't know." She looked down at her phone as if the answer might pop up on the screen. It didn't, and we continued on down the street.

"Babe!"

"What?"

"You can't reject an idea unless you provide an alternative."

"I did."

"No."

"I said, Another Kind."

"But that was before I said pizza. Pizza was my alternative to your idea, so now it's your turn again."

Did she really not know how this worked? I thought.

"I said I don't care. You can pick whatever you want."

"Oh gee, thanks."

This wasn't going well. I was just about to turn the car around and head home.

"Ok, pizza is fine," A note of exasperation was in her voice. Her head turned toward the window so I could just glimpse the silent mouthing of some extra words. "Jerk" perhaps.

Six words can lead to couples not speaking to each other. They are "where do you want to eat?" The words seem harmless enough. A simple inquiry. But the meaning behind the words is far more ominous: "Tell me where we are eating and pick something that will please me!" That's what we really want to say.

Why does the issue of meal planning cause us so much strife?

The anger: "you never pick where we are going to eat!"

The frustration: "just pick a place for once!"

The bitterness: "I'm going to get heartburn tonight because we ate so damn late because you took forever to make up your mind!"

When we were dating, all we did was eat. And it was never hard. We'd feast at some roadside hole in the wall and smack our lips like it was a Michelin-star restaurant. Each meal was better than the last. Our taste buds were blinded by love; we ate and ate, and nobody asked why, when, or where.

But here we are. Kids at home wondering what's for dinner while we drive aimlessly through the streets of town, bickering over food choices that we used to decide without so much as a second thought. Something happened along the way to cause us to get angry at each other for not being able to do something that we can't do ourselves - pick a place to eat! The whole thing is ridiculous.

We drove for a few more minutes in silence. I thought about these dopey arguments. We were fueled by hunger more than anything else. And I thought about the egg rolls and noodles at Another Kind. She was right. That actually was a good choice; sadly, we could have been there by now had I only listened. Instead, we are still hungry and still driving and driving and driving.

I turned down Main Street. I was getting desperate. The clock was ticking, and we were both ready to throw in the towel and go home and heat up some leftovers.

But then, I saw it like a beacon in the night sky. My saving grace! I yanked the wheel to the curb and brought the car to a sudden stop. She looked up from her phone, startled. The glow of the neon sign filled the car with blue and green light. Mongkut Thai!

Thai food was our first date; it had been our go-to for many a meal. We both loved it, and it never got old. I smiled. "Is Thai ok?"

"Sure." She smiled back.

I climbed out of the car feeling good. We had solved the dinner riddle. But, even better, tomorrow night: it would be her turn to pick the restaurant!

breakthrough

by Sharon Voorhees

after a gathering of
    cumulus clouds,
raindrops sprinkle
    on the thirsty soil

a weightless release
    of rainfall comes
forcing the water
    to soak the earth

in a singular moment
    clouds dissipate,
a cool breeze comes
    and the warm sun reappears

another breakthrough

Young Mother Project

by Sherrill A. Erickson

We had a studio apartment upstairs with a hot plate. Pictures of waves taped on the wall. My husband striding with the surfers, carrying his board.

In an empty jam jar, a daisy on the windowsill.

"Are you okay?"

It was my neighbor. Royden. He had been wounded in some war and limped. I nodded.

"Did he hurt you?"

I shook my head.

The lines on the side of his mouth. An old pretty boy. Still pretty. Seeing what he saw.

I didn't even get up off the floor. My hair had grown fast during the pregnancy.

"Don't cry."

The moods of the sea out the window. Every shade of blue, black, and grey. Cobalt.

Light slanting on the floor. Green glazed dragon tongues wrapping the ceramic hash pipe.

Crying, like everything else, runs out and dries up.

He handed me a folded white handkerchief.

"You have your baby to think about."

There was a quaver in his voice that old people have. The way he pronounced the word *baby*. "Going to California" guitar strumming a soundtrack from some other open window on the street.

Sun splashing through. The wafting curtain. Bong smoke. I made us toast and scrambled eggs. Scraping yellow butter. Coffee black bitter liquid. Real cream.

My nineteen-year-old husband bright as a rising sun. I covered him with my body. Laying back across his abdomen naked, my hair flowing over the side of the bed. He slid his fingers through pieces of it, looking into my eyes. I don't think I ever loved him more than I did at that moment. Kick of his heart throbbing in his parted lips with the sea having entered him while he surfed, living water. I would do anything. Be anything. Say anything. In that moment there was nothing else.

We made no plans.

If I lose you, I lose my life. Softness of your head. Baby hair. Little blanket. My arms. A baby crying. I'm here now. My feathers cover you. The miracle of warm milk. Your mouth will water like the tides moving. You have no teeth.

What I see is everything. Your hair on your head, most precious. To cut it. The first clipped lock saved in an envelope. I remember that time the van broke down and the engine stopped. How he pulled onto the shoulder. Walked with the gas can along the empty highway, disappearing. Our father.

With you in my arms and the ruffle of the wind. Your hair sweet in my lips, rustling tessellations of the desert grasses stirred in the air sweeping down from distant arid mountains bobbing little stars of flowers. I put my mouth on your cheek, and the fingers of your baby hand held my thumb. My song breath soft in virgin air. Crunch of dry sand under the sole of my shoes. We stood still to feel the beams of sun so generously bestowed.

What happened was that after a while, he was with someone else. I suspected it, and I was right. He got high with her in his van. And then he was gone with her. After my heart imploded and died, I fought for life. For an identity.

I wrote. The texture of the paper was a feeling. A scent. And the pencil, the thick pencil. The softness of the lead, the smudge of it darkening the paper, making letters. Decisions.

And with you asleep, I walked down the stairs onto main street that night. My blouse off the shoulder. Boots with heels.

Fluffed up hair. Backcombed on top. Powder, eyeliner, mascara, lipstick. You can wear a lot of make-up and still look subtle.

Just as I was leaving—for some reason—I looked up and saw Royden cracking his door. Why didn't he move to Laguna? Huntington was no place for him. He must like the surfer boys a lot. To put up with it.

"Can you watch her? I'll be right back."

"Where're you going?"

"She's asleep. I'll be right back."

Main Street. Ocean tongues. Engine oil. Highway shriek obliterated by the waves crushing themselves on their own blown froth, smell of the sea. Meat hissing over flames. This is the beach. This is the pier. Somewhere out here. This night. My boots in my hand. Running. I have dimes, nickels, pennies. Bought a bag of fries to shiver with. Heat and salt grease warm the paper bag. Ice in a cup. Just wanted something cold now. Worked there but nobody remembered. Before she was born. Maybe can go back. Part time.

A couple guys, teeth in beards.

"Hey baby."

He would be at the Golden Bear. I walked in. Stood in the crowded darkness. People. Wolf laughs. Loud music.

She was sitting on his lap. They didn't see me, and I ran away. Across blurred highway. To the empty beach. In front of the ocean, I convulsed with the swells. Communed with the booming thunder kings.

I wasn't drunk.

Royden was sitting in the chair when I got back. She was still asleep.

I was grabbing things. Stuffing everything in the army surplus bag. Cracked dishes. The jar, daisy dumped out. Baby food. Blankets, diapers.

"You have a place to go?"

Just then I heard my husband on the stairs. His key in the door.

I shoved the duffel bag under the bed.

To love him was an exercise in insanity, internal logic notwithstanding. It was grabbing at sea spray, shoved to the blind bottom beneath monster waves, one on top of the other. He took in the scene. Royden. Me all dressed up and emotional looking. You. Asleep. All nine pounds of you. Royden took his cue and departed.

"Meeting someone?"

"Just went for a walk."

"Dressed like a slut?"

He pulled his shirt over his head. A bruise on his neck. Her scent on him. I slid my hands into his belt, my fingers finding his zipper as he told me, "I don't want that faggot near my baby."

When he fell asleep, I got up and pulled out the duffel wedged under the bed, gently lifted my baby to my chest, heavy and warm.

I tapped on Royden's door.

He opened it. Saw me.

Where does love begin and where does it end? Is it something from the sea, full of sea juice and sea squirt? Ions in metal blood? Sparks bursting into night sky? Condensing whorls of your stamped fingertips?

How do I protect you when I can't protect myself? My running legs and the ceaseless throb of my wanting. When I reach. Is it an arm? A throat? A deeper pit? Is it hunger?

What is hunger?

The Day Before My Father Stopped Dying and Died

by Laura Miller

The day before my father stopped dying and died
I had an unprecedented argument
with my Mother,
well within his ear shot.

The last time
he heard our voices
and the first time
he heard my anger.

All the years he's been gone
I worried that this
was a bitter moment
he took to eternity.

Or does he rest easy?
Pleased to see himself in me
when I show some spunk.

"You never have to change anything you got up in the middle of the night to write."

—Saul Bellow

i beg of you
by Marissa C. Knox

you.
you have not seen what I've seen.
done
what I've done.
felt or known or touched
what I've touched, known, and felt.

you,
who is too busy for a phone call.

you,
who has too much to worry about.

you,
who doesn't have time to listen.

you,
who rushes from one thing to the next.

you,
who is not available to connect.

you.

you have not witnessed
the vibrant sun
silently announce
the shimmering possibilities of this day
by painting swirls of pink and gold
into the foam of a whispering wave.

you have not tasted
the bright orange nasturtium
growing in the green house.

you have not heard
the enthusiasm
and conversation amongst the pine trees
in the wind.

you have not touched,
have not pressed
your hands and feet
into the sun-warmed stones
by the cool, flowing water.

you have not known
the purple joy
of lupines resting
in the shade
of an aspen grove.

you have not felt
the velvet moss
on the fallen log
beside the clear river.

you have not jumped,
have not leapt off a black rock
into the sparkling, turquoise depths
among the sea turtles.

you have not rested
at the top of a mountain
as a rainbow emerged
from the misty clouds.

you have not seen
the swallowtail butterfly
flicker with bliss,
as she drinks the nectar
from the pink phlox
under the glow of twilight.

you have not smelled
the soothing sweetness
of jasmine
in the soft,
milky light
of the moon.
you have not been immersed
in awe
while gazing at billions of twinkling stars
in divine intimacy with the cosmos.

Oh, I beg of you,
dear one.

stop.

s l o w   down.
be. still.

sense.

feel.

know.

breathe in

and

breathe out.

receive
the blessings
and gifts of this
wildly precious life.

do not squander
what you are holding
in this very moment.

be a space
for the mystery
of life to unfold
within your presence,
like steam
drifting through fresh air.

turn your palms up
and remember.

i beg of you.

Inspired by a poetry exercise led by MaryAnn Easley based on an excerpt from "Don't Give Me Advice" by Luis Marin, Tompkins Square CRW

Surf's Up

by Anna Jevne

There I was, in 1971, thirty years old and dressed to the nines, standing in the crowded ballroom of the Beverly Hilton Hotel. My husband and I had donated money to a charity. This noisy black-tie party was our ear-splitting reward. While the band pounded out its crazy throbs, I kept a phony smile on my face and spoke to our circle of friends in vapid dribble.

Why did we go to these things?

After a while, the band stopped playing. We could hear again. Like all big parties, everybody began circulating. Two happy-looking fellas joined our small group. I recognized Jerry immediately. I hadn't seen him in years.

"Well, here's someone I'll never forget," he said, turning to everybody while acknowledging me with a slight and somewhat regal bow that sent heads spinning. What in the world was this stranger talking about? I received a quizzical glance from my husband.

"How do you know Anna?" someone asked.

"That woman marked me forever," Jerry said with a smirk on his face.

The group went silent. *What had Anna done?* Was it something unseemly? Something very un-black tie?

My heart sank. Was Jerry going to tell everybody how stupid and crazy we were as teenagers? Did he intend to spill the beans about that particularly wild and magical moment we shared? All while I was trying to look and act sophisticated?

With a sly smile on his face and a wink toward me, he leaned down, lifted the cuff of his tuxedo pants leg and slowly raised the fabric as high as his knee. A six-inch long, two-inch wide, deep scar ran straight down Jerry's shin. Everybody gasped at the sight.

Right then, I knew what caused the injury. I remembered seeing blood streaming down Jerry's ankle and seeping into the sand after his second heroic try.

We were fifteen at the time, too young to drive. Vacationing on Balboa Island, Jerry and I never made plans, but somehow, he would always find me. Either I was coming back from racing my sailboat or sitting under my umbrella on the Apolena beach knitting argyle socks.

"Come on out," he'd say.

Off we'd go.

Jerry had a ten-foot, blue Wizard outboard motorboat.

The sky was bright blue that summer afternoon. We zipped past the Newport Jetty and began splashing our way down the coast. We hadn't gone far when Jerry pointed out the long, shiny, ocean-green tubes of waves rolling toward Little Corona Del Mar beach. "Let's have some fun," he said. He goosed the engine and zipped the boat up to the top of one of the waves. To my wild delight, he sped along its crest. Just before the wave was about to break, he ducked the boat down behind the mountain of moving water, and we slipped away.

"That was crazy," Jerry cried out.

I laughed.

"Let's do it again," he said.

Over and over, wave after wave, up and down we went. Every time we topped the towering crest of a wave, I could see the kids sitting on the beach and spot the heads of the body surfers popping up and down in the churning foam roaring toward shore from the last breaking break. As we sped along the top of one giant wave, Jerry cried out, "Wanna do it?"

Standing there in that ballroom, I could still remember my answer. "Sure," I squealed in sheer delight.

What in the world were we thinking? We weren't.

Down the breaking wave we went. Buried in a wild fan of ocean spray, we shot straight toward the beach. After a peerless ride, the boat's bow knifed itself into the sandy shore with a dead thud. Still dry, I stepped onto the beach. "That was great," I yelled out.

A moment later, I spotted the lifeguard climbing down his beach-chair tower. He didn't look happy. Holding a life preserver with one hand, and scratching his mop of thick, sun-bleached hair with the other, he walked up to us and announced, "You're not allowed to land boats on this beach."

"We just did," I told him. I remember thinking that was a really *smart quip* on my part. How stupid could I get? "Take that thing right back out into the ocean," he growled at us. "If you don't, I'm going to be in trouble." I never understood his logic on that point, but we were cooperative kids in the fifties. While he and everybody on the beach watched us, Jerry settled me down in the bow of the boat. He gave the stern a shove in the wild hope of pushing his little blue Wizard back out into the open ocean.

"Go, Jerry, go," I heard someone yell from the beach.

The surf never stops. A thick layer of foam from one of the bigger waves thundered toward the shore. Its force lifted the bow of the boat into the air. Jerry lost his grip on the stern. I jumped out. The wild lather threw me back on the beach. Drenched, I watched the boat swirl in the surf while Jerry chased it. The boat landed on the sand next to me. Jerry washed ashore behind it.

By now, a big crowd was standing at the water's edge, and a few of the most determined body-surfer kids offered to help Jerry make a second try.

"You sit down here and wait," Jerry said to me. "Once I get the boat beyond the waves, swim out and meet me."

I did what I was told and snuggled down next to the lifeguard. I remember thinking he was cute. We watched as eight body surfer kids and Jerry made a second attempt to push the boat out toward the ocean. They didn't get far. Another wave sent a wall of foam at least two feet thick straight at them. Terrified, the guys, and Jerry, let the boat go and dove under the raging suds. The boat flew in the air, flipped over, and came whirling back onto the beach with the propeller in the air.

The noisy Hilton Hotel band started playing again.

Only then, at that moment, did I realize that Jerry had been dreadfully injured and never told me. "The propeller!" I screamed over the music. "The blades sliced down your leg, didn't they?"

"Yes," Jerry called back. He carefully returned the leg of his tuxedo to its proper place.

After seeing Jerry's scar, the group demanded the story behind it. Near the end of his telling, someone asked, "How did you get the boat off the beach?"

Jerry's bravado sagged. "We called for a truck," he admitted. His voice sounded flat. "The guys helped me carry it up that fifty-foot rocky bluff to the road above."

"That alone is an accomplishment," someone said.

Jerry shook his head. I could tell by his expression that he didn't think so. He turned to leave, but then, with a quick turn, he stepped back and whispered in my ear, "Was it worth it?"

"It sure was," I murmured back.

"Would you do it again?"

"In a minute."

Hearing that, he walked off, sporting the swagger he always had. I watched as he disappeared into the elegant crowd. I never saw him again.

My husband was furious with me for the rest of the evening.

Fighting with Form

by Margaret de Jaham

Try to write haiku
Five and seven syllables
Counting on fingers.

The frustration grows
Six syllable lines abound
Each a masterpiece.

Struggling to find
Elusive beat of seven
Time to take a break.

Rearrange the art
Every piece in different place
How it all seems new!

What shall I do now?
Search where inspiration lies
Walk in the garden.

Time for mindfulness
Admire the plants and flowers
Take some photographs.

Notice the colors
The changing slant of sunlight
All the shades of green.

This starts to make sense
Constraints of form are helpful
Satisfaction grows.

Creeping crepuscule
Yet another change of pace
Time for cocktail hour.

Momentum of Manner

by John Henning

Ahhh, the release, release
Such euphoric release
From, torment, torment, torment…
Incessant surreal torment.
Ahhh, the surcease, surcease
Such ecstatic surcease
From, discontent, discontent, discontent
Discordant lethal discontent
But, by manner of release
By corporeal, by ethereal
Momentum, beyond surcease
Compels descent, impels ascent

"Either write something worth reading or do something worth writing."

—*Benjamin Franklin*

A Fish Story

by Deberah Porter

In the summer of '72, my parents took me to Cape Cod to celebrate my graduation from law school.

My family didn't have much money, so we stayed at the Motel 6 in East Falmouth. We enjoyed bowls of clam chowder, the hotel pool, and especially the beach. Being without means, we'd never had many vacations. This short holiday was the best gift ever.

Worried my class ring would slip off my finger, I put it on my necklace. The heavy ring bounced on my chest as I moved about. A reminder of my accomplishment.

I romped in the water, took long jogs on the beach, and stared at the ocean contemplating how my college degree would guarantee a good-paying job. I wanted to reimburse my family for all they'd done to help me through school. Even with an undergrad scholarship, law school had been expensive as well as difficult.

While splashing in the ocean, I lost my class ring. I was crushed...it had taken me two part-time jobs to pay for it. My red stone ring of pride was lost forever.

After I returned from the Cape, my high hopes for a meaningful career were limited. So many grads made competition stiff in the workforce. I passed the bar but there were too many lawyers out of work already. Instead, I toiled in a low-paying job working as a clerk in a small law office, hoping they'd eventually find a spot for me as a junior lawyer. My family continued to struggle to make ends meet.

Almost a year went by. Then a mysterious small package arrived from Virginia. I opened it immediately. Inside was a note from a man with his phone number.

He'd found my ring.

I called to thank him. "Hello, this is Maria Zappa. You were kind enough to return my class ring. Thank you so much. You're quite the detective. How did you find me?"

"No problem. I looked up your initials and year from your Harvard ring and guessed, since there was only one female with your initials."

"Where did you find it? And what are these other items you sent? I don't understand."

"Well, true story. I found your ring in the belly of a fish."

"A fish? What?"

"Yeah, well, I'm no fisherman. I'm a lawyer and went to Harvard myself. I was out on a half-day boat off the Cape and caught the biggest catch of the day. It was a fluke really. Me catching a big fish."

"What kind of fish?"

"A big barracuda."

"Okay, so what about the other items? Why did you send them to me?"

"Since they were in the same fish, I assumed all to be yours. When they gutted the fish, I found your monogrammed ring, a slimy dime, and a wad of cash wrapped with a thick rubber band. Oh, I took one of the bills to pay for shipping. Hope that's okay?"

"Okay? Kind sir, you have no idea what this means to me. The ring is precious for many reasons. The money is sorely needed, and well, the dime, I guess I can always make a phone call."

I thanked him again and put the tarnished ring, now missing the red stone, on my finger. Before I hung up, I asked, "So, does your firm need a young lawyer?"

Cabin in the Woods

by Jade Marie Smith

I will no longer be your cabin in the woods
The place you think you own because you paid other people
   to build it
The place you visit every few months when you feel there's
   nowhere else to go
I will no longer be your outlet or your escape
I will no longer be your cabin in the woods
I am not a second house in your life but a home within myself
I am not an object you hide under your bed to leave
   forgotten until you remember again
I am not yours anymore, but I am myself within
I will not allow you to take control when you please
Today I realize I am not yours or anyone else's property
I am not a cabin in the woods.
P.S. I love you.

"Individually, we are one drop. Together, we are an ocean."
—*Ryunosuke Satoro*

bell against bears

by Chris Perry

a day so fine.
missing the steep ravine, we climbed to
the summit and backtracked, surfing in
neutral, taking a left to a cozy dead end,
and parked precariously on a slope. the
trail was slight and crazy, tilted as it was
at an absurd degree --- with three-petaled
purple flowers and scrubby tufts of grass
the color of copper's patina and normal
rust on retaining mesh and outlet pipes as
witnesses. oaken copses, berimmed with
lichen, cooled us. we galloped to stinson:
why not? there was a gossiping gathering
of agave, variegated and wormrotten,
but delightful to live inside of. the grass
was flooded, ankle-sucking, so we had a
chocolate malt (a chocolate malt!) and
sat on a picnic bench with feet held up.
you wrote notes for your novel, while i
marveled at how ridiculous i am. on the
death march back to the car, we ran,
because it was just as difficult, but faster.
the sun was setting. we hid in a bramble
just off the path. we swore we'd never hike
again without you in a skirt.

storyline

by Paula Shaffer Robertson

i have longed to tell the story of a motherless child,
a letter of love to a woman unknown, yet deified,
who comes to me in daylight dreams, so personable,
visceral impulse, internal fear, reinvent the lost, those
long hopeless dreams, the woman i loved from a
distant sphere; that beautiful face so mysterious,
eyes that pierce into emptiness, undoing time; the cold,
motherless charm, rooted into this heart, stranded, alone.

in my earlier days, hope was a theme that drove me
to strive; but now i am aged, and reality tears down
the essence of pain, the ugliness stripped down to the
core of extreme; i cannot write without cowering within,
from the shame of belonging to no one; unclaimed; knowing
worthlessness reigns, self-doubt unchained; who am i
now in your shadow's refrain, no trace of your voice, touch,
or your heart's claim; a shell of life, your imprinted bloodstain.

Me   Wo Man

by Olivia Starace

Where is that fire in the belly
That pounding heart?
Put it down girl…   girl?
The words, I mean!
Let them leak out of the pen!

Come on,
What are you afraid of?
Wild gypsy…let your spirit
Be free like your ash hair…

                          Wild!

Even in age   it's in there
You naked young/old
Brown   barefoot woman

Do It!   Write!
Quit taming your old words
The spit stains
Your wrong rhyming words

Be that   WO   MAN!
That hairy gorilla
Pounding its chest
With its fist

Don't forget the   PASSION!
The blood   the dance
The dirt…. really?
The dirt?

Where are the splinters
From the yoke that you carry?
Like the cracked egg?   Like the brain?
Initially   soft boiled   over easy
Life   scrambled   fried

Where is the Judas kiss
Where is the hammer   the nails?
The Crucifixion?
No   one   person   wants   THE   dirt

The brain now shows
It's sunny side up
while she walks on the unshaded side of the road
Wild ash-grey hair now combed and in place
With manicured hands in her pockets

Remembering
The passion   the blood   THE   dirt
You   wild   young/old   shameless   WO MAN

W R I T E!!!

"Substitute 'damn' every time you're inclined to write 'very;' your editor will delete it and the writing will be just as it should be."

—Mark Twain

Tribute to Oka-san

by Setsuko Takemura

as the wind blows in silence
bounteous clouds hover over
not just the white, but the azures, ochres
and the misty shades
then like the ashes
they dissipate into the lonely darkness
and then return again for us to gaze upon
like the memories
to share with friends once known

That Crooked Smile

by Carol Ann Merker

My husband Ron and I owned a dive shop for many years. Ron ran the shop and regularly offered scheduled boat trips to Catalina Island for the scuba divers. I felt lucky to join these trips.

The kelp forest found off our California coast makes our Channel Islands very unique. It is beautiful to see underwater, and it is home to an abundance of sea life.

On our boat trips, some divers would take game such as fish, scallops, and abalone. Some were interested in underwater photography. Others would enjoy exploring and watching what would swim past them that day.

One October, Ron offered an underwater Pumpkin Carving Contest. Those interested were to bring a pumpkin and carving tools.

As a certified diver with more than ten years of experience, I wanted to try something new. This event would test my diving skills and creativity. I decided to enter the contest.

After shopping for an appropriately sized and shaped pumpkin and searching my kitchen for the proper tools, I was excited to go on this dive.

The boat skipper anchored the boat in an area along the coast with varying depths for all to enjoy.

I prepared for my dive.

Suited up.

Compressed air turned on.

Mesh bag attached to my weight belt.

I placed the pumpkin and carving tools into the mesh bag—all set.

I put on my swim fins and mask at the boat's exit. With one hand on my mask, I took a giant stride off the boat into the water.

Descending to about 25 feet, I needed to make myself neutrally buoyant by adjusting my BC (buoyancy compensator). If I was neutrally buoyant, I would be hanging in the water, not going up, not going down. But I still felt too buoyant, so I added a couple of rocks from the nearby ledge to the front pocket of my BC vest. That helped.

I put my pumpkin on the flattest rock I could find, hoping to avoid a Humpty-Dumpty event. I was ready to carve.

The long, sharp, pointy knife suddenly looked menacing to me as I swayed back and forth in the constant shallow water surge. Finally, everything was aligned, so I quickly cut off the top. I started scooping out the pulp when I noticed it floating upward.

Surprise! A large school of small fish suddenly appeared to help with the cleanup. No more cleanup was needed underwater, thanks to the helpful fish.

My biggest challenge then was to keep myself and the pumpkin steady as I carved. Looking around, I found a rock that fit inside the empty pumpkin to help it stay in place.

I prepared to carve the face. The eyes and nose took longer to cut than I'd imagined. I check my gauges for air and time. I was okay.

Then, for the mouth.

A smile is a challenging cut. I began and almost had the perfect smile when the knife slid halfway up the pumpkin's face. Whoops!

I finished the smile and looked at my pumpkin-turned jack-o-lantern. Oh, well, good enough for the first try.

Upon ascending, the divers placed their jack-o-lanterns along the boat railing. I took a look.

Mine was not the prettiest nor the scariest, but everyone laughed the hardest when they saw that crooked smile.

Haunt Me

by Sherrill A. Erickson

I'm walking through the fields
Dry summer grasses gone to seed
Let the shadow of the bird above me
Be you

When the leaves rustle in whooshes of air
Let it quicken me in the evening
When I walk alone

When the ocean splatters
Foams, slurps, and slides, plate over plate of liquid
Let it be you
Laughing

Haunt me
When I'm driving home at night
Be the red eyes my headlights hit in the forest
Some wild animal
Watching

Haunt me
Never let me rest
Beat me with your winds
Strangle me in vines
Bury me and blacken my bones to coal
Burn me
Let the fire be you
Torch in your hands
Let your face be superimposed on everything I see
Your Voice every sound

Every word, every noise, every note of music
All the electric fibers within, particles of me
Let them all resonate with your haunting, your ghost, your eyes
Your dark, steady eyes
That seem to hold me, and smile
That seem to know
That seem

Kind

"The purpose of a writer is to keep civilization from destroying itself."

—*Albert Camus*

Abatement

by John T. Knox

Cigarette butt
Bottle cap
Plastic straw
Candy wrapper
Disposable facemask

Got my bag, bucket, gloves, grabber.
"Thank you for doing that," I hear.
"You're very welcome," I reply.
I get acknowledged.
It spurs me on . . .

Hot Cheetos bag
Starbucks stopper
Capri Sun pouch
Chick-Fil-A carton
Red Bull can

That one is recyclable. Goes in the bucket.
Worst are the parking lots. Along curbs.
Public parks. Around benches. Under picnic tables.
Wherever humans pass, and gather.
Abatement of litter. Needed.

Busted balloon
Hope the party was good . . .
Crushed ketchup packet
Squirted on a burger, fries, hot dog?
Stained popsicle stick
Skeletal remains of a sweet something
Used floss pick
Teeth kept clean but . . . the Earth?
Crystal Geyser bottle, still half-full
Pour it out. Pop it in the bucket.

Unwanted things. Cast down.
Blown around. Trapped in gutters, planters, low shrubs.
Always, there is more.
Ugly human refuse.
Often hiding, hard to see . . . unless you look.

Dog poop . . . in a poop bag!
How nice! Now two pollutants, instead of one!
Old condom
Wonder if they had a good time . . .
Vaping kit
Better not let parents see that!
Banana peel
Leave that there. Biodegradable.
Styrofoam cup
Bad guy. Get him. Not biodegradable.

What must the birds think? Flying above it.
Or the bugs? Crawling under it.
Or the fish? Swimming among it.
The throw-downs go to where it's low.
Into crevices. Bodies of water. Breaking apart. Insidious bits.

Another cigarette butt
On the ground . . . where all the butts seem to go.
Another bottle cap
Budweiser this time. Gateway to a cheap buzz.
Another plastic straw
What the hell? Was this ever used?
Another candy wrapper
Taffy bites. "Airheads." Apt name. For users.
Another disposable facemask
Despised. Discarded. Disdainfully.

People pushing strollers, walking dogs,
jogging, cycling . . . pass by.
"Awesome job," I hear.
"Thank you for saying that," I reply.
Soldiering on. For sanitation.

Yet another cigarette butt . . .

"I'm not the smartest fellow in the world, but I sure can pick smart colleagues."

—Franklin D. Roosevelt

Love Letters

by Julie Crandall

My dad held the letter and stared, touching the blue ink that was unfazed by the sixty-five years since it had been written and the envelope torn open for the first time. Tears flowed down his cheeks as we sat close together on his front porch, breathing in the warm late summer air—everything around us—the foothills, the palm trees, the bright Jacarandas cast soft shadows. Dad scanned the weathered envelope: a purple 3-cent stamp, the postmark from Redlands, CA, April 5, 1955. It was addressed to my grandparents:

Mr. & Mrs. J.H. McClelland
1714 Mar Vista
Pasadena, Calif.

Her loopy handwriting was instantly recognizable, never changing throughout her life.

Dad's hands trembled slightly as he struggled to get the letter out of the envelope; maybe it was the Parkinson's, perhaps the thrill of remembering.

The rows of Mom's left-handed cursive with all of its arcs and swirls were too small for Dad to read, so he handed the letter to me.

Dear mother and dad,

I'm sorry I haven't written sooner but boy - have I been busy....Sonny called me tonight, and we are going to triple date to the dance and then afterward, we are going to Palm Springs. Sounds like fun!

"Sonny!" Dad grumbled and his face contorted to a jealous disgust.

"Wait, Dad, listen..."

I found out a few days ago that a fellow named Jack Black

wants to take me out. It was a big mystery because only my girlfriend seemed to know who he is and so finally today, I saw him for the first time. What a doll he is!

"She said that?" Dad's body seemed to lift from his slouch instantly, and his eyes brightened; his face held all the expressiveness that his disease and circumstances had wiped away. The years evaporated.

He's a Pi Chi and probably drinks up with the other members. But I would like to go out with him at least once.

Dad tossed his head back, squinting with laughter I hadn't seen in a long time. Suddenly the "bad boy" look I remembered from childhood replaced the face of the 84-year-old man in hospice care. He threw his arms up in the air, and with a half laugh and half wail, Dad spoke in the direction of the heavens, "Let me die now!"

There were six letters. Mom's voice, her energy, and her spirit emerged from the paper we held. And here was Dad, clutching Mom again. We read and reread them, analyzing every nuance, wondering what might have happened if he had never gotten the courage to ask her out. Or what if she stayed with her boyfriend, Sonny? Or what if that first date didn't go well?

How easily life might have twisted in another direction.

"If everything didn't happen exactly as it did in these letters, I wouldn't exist. Every one of us is an against-all-odds-miracle."

We stared at each other as we thought about that. Then more tears. Cathartic tears. Tears of wonder and thanks and pain and loss.

The letters had been discovered several months earlier. Dad had come home from the hospital, and I'd flown out wondering if this might be the last time I'd see him. I sat next to him, watching his chest rise and fall, listening to the sound of his breath.

Suddenly, his eyes shot open, and he looked straight at me, "Did you check the safe deposit box?"

I stared back, confused.

"Did you? Did you check it?" This time with more urgency.

"Don't worry, Dad, I will," With that, his eyes were again closed.

A few weeks passed by before I mentioned it to my sister-in-law.

"Maybe there's something in there he wants you to get." So the next time they visited, they slipped into the bank, signed the ledger, and with a twist of the key, they opened the safe deposit box to find a zip lock bag tucked way in the back with six old letters bearing Mom's familiar handwriting.

Dad declined over the following months, but those letters always sparked stories of the old days, unfiltered and filled with a once-forgotten exuberance.

A couple of times, Dad would think he remembered where more letters were hidden. We'd go on a scavenger hunt around the house. A secret safe here, a locked closet there. Once Dad's eyes lit up, "They're in the attic."

I loved Dad's sense of adventure and intrigue, but the attic was a no-go, a dangerous booby trap. If you can make it up the creaky pull-down "stairs," good luck when you get to the top. If the spiders don't get you, the nails poking through from the roof definitely will.

"I'm going up!" Dad said as he shuffled toward the door with his walker. We laughed and had to talk him out of climbing up into the attic himself. He had six letters. They would have to be enough.

After Dad died, several old crumbling boxes tucked

away in the booby-trapped attic were discovered. Inside were hundreds of old letters. They trace their first date in 1955 until they were married in 1959. It's an unfolding love story; the letters fit together like a puzzle, and two people emerge from the past.

Although I know the end of the story, I'm still on the edge of my seat, waiting to find out. Will Dad get into dental school? Will they get pinned before Mom leaves for Hawaii? How did Mom make it through school when she was having so much fun? How did Dad sneak his dissected pig out of the lab to study for his exam? It's profoundly absorbing.

I scour each letter looking for clues that reveal both the new and the familiar, climbing into a world to discover a version of my parents when they were the age of my youngest son. I find myself adoring my dad as if I'm once again a little girl; while discovering parts of my mom that make my 55-year-old eyes widen at the college girl she was.

There's a scent to the paper that I wonder if they smelled. The crisp stationery on my fingertips began its journey on their fingertips when these letters were passed back and forth between my parents' hands, ink pouring from pens that lay on their desks.

Sometimes I laugh as I read. And sometimes I cry. Love letters create a space where time becomes fuzzy, and love feels eternal.

Dear Carole

I've been studying chem so much that it's coming out my ears $c+s2 \sim> cs2+3cl \sim> ccl4$ and I even dream of it at night. If I don't get a C in there, I'll really be mad. It's really hot today and I'd like to hit the rays, but I'd better cram it up. Last night I was accidentally looking at a little TV and saw Nat King Cole. So he sang when you fall in love & it really made me lonesome as anything for you. I almost cried, except my folks were there.

Well, that's about it. I'm pale as anything and have a mild case of something or other.

   Miss you.
   Love you lots
   Jack

"I can shake off everything as I write; my sorrows disappear, my courage is reborn."

—Anne Frank

I see you, disappearing

by Kimberly Krantz

Like the sun slipping below the horizon
Like the mountain-top trees being swallowed by the fog
Like the childhood friend who moves away
Like the White Rhino before taking its last run
Like the struggle to breathe when the body is tired and worn.

the change

by Paula Shaffer Robertson

i am constantly fanning myself
although menopause ended ages ago
a certain fertility i never knew

a possession of inconsolable grief
slowly seeping into this heart's core
when life felt her immense possibilities

taken away

as eggs released ceased to mature
a life meant to be that never was
a character uncharacterized

the death of dreams immortalized
as silent tears refuse to shed
sleek silver stains imbedded deep

bereft

i hear the laughter of a child at play
with a mother immersed in joyous wonder
at the spawn of her – this – miraculous gift

that gift of life as an unending abattoir
of dreams unfurled in didactic sequence
of what will never be stone cold reality

numbing chill

a reminder that life itself is flesh and water,
faith and disbelief, unmitigated joy, incessant grief,
a cacophony of dissonance unresolved

Fourteen

by Mark Van Houten

"Just 14 mgs are all the psychiatrist wants you to take. Just 14 mgs," pleaded Justin's mother, juggling the car steering wheel and her desire to make eye contact. Justin turned his scowl through the passenger window. He gazed toward the distant dark horizon lined with silhouetted trees that cleaved to reveal a brilliantly defiant moon. *My soul is a moon-spirit,* thought Justin. He frowned at the specter of misty clouds and encircling ravens that threatened to encroach upon his indomitable moon. Justin's brave moon-spirit inspired his resolve to refuse psych meds that he judged would smother his soul to mitigate his public shame.

But not for Father Timothy. He, with his beady, vacuous eyes, beaked nose, and slicked-back, black hair, flapping his pious arms so sanctimoniously, after touching me privately again. And again.

Justin's mother scanned the car radio to find something to calm Justin's fidgety hands and darting eyes, but Justin hears only the number fourteen on the music charts. He sees 10:14 on his wristwatch. He knows the day is the fourteenth. The perplexing repetition of fourteens rattles around in Justin's mind.

Fourteen in the meds, the car radio, my watch, and I'm fourteen. The edginess in Justin's mind swirled around the dizzying dance of fourteens.

Justin's private reverie ends abruptly. A black raven crashed the windshield. His mother slammed the car brakes, snapping the seatbelt harness, that knotted Justin's neck taut like an imprisoning straight jacket.

In the car's immediate path searing red flashes shot from an improvised roadblock sign. Bridge closed, it said. Follow detour signs for the next 14 miles. Justin clawed his neck free from the seatbelt's suffocating grip. He sucked air. A jittery fluttering in his gut convinced him that this babble of fourteens was just like the creeping mist and encroaching ravens, portending some evil curse, perhaps a fateful reckoning, just ahead.

The bridge was desolate, save for a police squad car light spinning and pulsing. Mom talked to the policeman. *Maybe something about the dead raven. Or maybe something about Father Timothy.* Justin imagines that the raven intentionally blocked his escape at the detour sign, so the police could ensnare him into custody, and imprison him into shameful isolation. *A prison of psych drugs and guilt.* Justin envisioned the blistering, judgmental glare of Father Timothy's eyes shifting blame. Justin's disappointed parents retreating, palpably ashamed. Illuminated on the inside of his eyelids he saw visions of a spiraling, fiery abyss administering punishment for his sinful damnation.

The policeman glares inquisitorially at Justin. The cruiser's number looks something like a fourteen, so Justin knows that the policeman knows that Justin is escaping punishment and is coming for him. Panicked, he rips the seat belt from his body, bolts from the car, and tears across the darkened threshold of the bridge. His legs power frantically past each of the thirteen bridge struts. He stops at the fourteenth.

"Climb, Justin. Climb" A deafening cacophony of ethereal voices implore him to ascend. Upward on the thin railing's ledge Justin wobbles precariously on slippery toes. His hair flutters. His heart skips. Yet, he bursts into giggles, when he looks down at the relentless torrent of the river rapids, beckoning, echoing up a call to freedom.

Judgment point. In Justin's catechism the innocent would have cowered. Their toes would have clawed at the edge of the bridge, too fearful to fly. The innocent would have entrusted their steadfast faith and soul to the Holy Father, nestling contritely in the confessional of Father Timothy.

Justin turned outward in and gazed into the heavens. *His touch pecked a hole in my blameless soul, from which only death can flow.* "Yes, for Jesus, only death could unlock his troubled soul" was the response.

Justin released a sanguine, soulful sigh, steaming seamlessly, effortlessly into the cold night air as a vaporized ghost, swaddling and comforting, as would the shroud of blessed baptismal blood, known only to martyrs. *Yes, martyrs.*

Justin shivered with the thrill of anticipation, of absolution, of liberation, of salvation, of rebirth. In the frigid darkness the welcoming embrace of gravity pulled him forward. He surrendered without misgivings. With wings uplifted, he swooned, as if in flight, already in heaven.

ONE, TWO, THREE: Descent hastens. The chill of the night air whistles across his burning cheeks. Holy water draws forth from his eyes.

FOUR, FIVE, SIX: Justin looks up. The lights along the bridge fade, but *the stars are like pearls.* Vivid in their crispness, they fill the black night air with angelic droplets of electricity.

SEVEN, EIGHT, NINE: Justin sees himself reflected like a mirror of the defiant moon awaiting him in the glassy sheen of the baptismal river below. *Cool waters to quench the fires of guilt.*

TEN, ELEVEN, TWELVE: Justin imagines himself a winged, transmogrified, celestial spirit, white and pure, hovering next to Jesus at the altar.

THIRTEEN: Justin poses as God's altar boy. *To you I raise my head. Close my eyes. Open my mouth. Offer out my tongue.*

FOURTEEN.

"Don't bend; don't water it down; don't try to make it logical; don't edit your own soul according to the fashion. Rather, follow your most intense obsessions mercilessly."

—Franz Kafka

Don't Mind Me

by MJ West

On the third day after my left knee replacement surgery, my knee is swollen three times the size of the other. Falling backward trying to get out of bed, I faint and land on the floor.

A few minutes after my husband Vern calls 911, I hear three paramedics run up the stairs to our bedroom. After taking my vitals and examining my knee, Rob, the head paramedic, tells me he thinks my fainting was pain induced.

Stooped over me, he asks if I want to go to the hospital.

"No. I have an appointment with my orthopedic surgeon tomorrow."

"Okay, I'll give you an injection for the pain." He turns and looks up at Vern. "Keep icing that knee, twenty minutes on, twenty minutes off."

I'm still lying on the floor, talking to him, when my daughter, Lisa bursts through the door.

"Mom! What's going on? Oh, hi Rob! I haven't seen you since high school graduation."

"Lisa." Smiling, he stands up and gives her a big hug. "What are you doing here?"

"I've come to see my mom. I live just around the corner."

"How's your sister Cari?"

While they continue to chat, the other two paramedics are gazing out of my bedroom window.

"Wow, what a view," one says.

"Yeah", the other says, "You can see the beach and the pier. Look, there's Dana Point."

Lisa bends down next to me on the floor and whispers, "Mom, can I make some coffee for the guys?"

"Sure, go right ahead. Don't mind me."

Puttin' on the Hair Shirt

by JG McCrillis

Just askin' me, myself, and I
"Self . . .
After so many repetitions, revisions, and twerks
Holding forth with your audience of one,
Did you get it right this time?
Make your point?
Give 'em a piece of your mind?
Cuss 'em out good?
Get in all your ripostes?
All those righteous retorts?
Put 'em on the straight and narrow?
Yes! you say
Ah, sweet vendetta.

So now, tell me
Who was it you were really talking
To when you were talking
To yourself."

"Ideas are like rabbits. You get a couple and learn how to handle them, and pretty soon you have a dozen."

—*John Steinbeck*

Guaranteed

by MaryAnn Easley

You will suffer, learn the hard way.
It's guaranteed you will disappoint
those you love, and be disappointed too,
that you will drop the ball, fumble the catch,
say the wrong thing, burn the whole batch.

You'll be scammed, fooled, conned, tricked,
embarrassed, humbled, tumbled, ashamed,
wrecked, wracked with regret, neglect, resentment,
you'll be rejected, refused, misused, excused,
abused, confused, bruised, and accused.

No, your dreams won't come true,
you're no Cinderella, only you, not a rising star.
You'll trip over your feet, fall flat on your face,
fail the test, miss the bus, forget to call.
No hero will stop bullets or break your fall.

Your 4,000 weeks will disappear, if you're lucky
enough to get those weeks, but there's no guarantee
you'll live forever, no insurance that any surgery,
procedure, or tonic will make you strong,
no assurance you'll stick around very long.

And so, my question is: what're you going to do
to escape the fear, disappear, use your time,
pay for the crime, spend your dime, stop the comet,
lift yourself higher, and all humanity too?
So, tell me, please . . .
in God's name, what the hell are you going to do?

No Wrong Turns
by Peggy Jaffe

Some call me brave, others call me crazy. At midlife, I followed my bliss and moved from California to the Tuscan countryside. As for crazy, meaning unprepared, that describes my first month residing here. It's so easy to fall in love with this scenic land. During prior visits, my husband, Norman, did all the driving. I try to picture myself traversing these tortuous roads when he returns to our California home in a few days. I'm petrified.

Italian law also limits me. Foreigners can buy real estate, even historical properties, but no vehicle, not even a three-wheeled Piaggio, until qualified for residency. I started the process, but it will be a while. So, here I am, living in Paradise, neighbors beyond earshot, and counting on others for transportation. Rental cars are available, but rarely with automatic transmission. I've never driven a stick shift. Starting here, on these ribbon-thin, corkscrew roads, is out of the question. There must be a rental car agency that can meet my requirements.

Meanwhile, our Italian connection, Olivia, made it possible to survive temporarily without a car. She introduced Norman and me to this area soon after purchasing property here six years ago. When her neighbor decided to sell what is now our House of Dreams, she notified us immediately and set up my support system; Lucia, valued for her culinary skills, and Bruno, Olivia's gardener. Since Olivia lives and works in Rome weekdays, she asked them to help with transportation until I lease a car.

* * * * *

Whenever Bruno takes me shopping, his black-spotted

hound, Teresa, comes along. She sprawls across the back seat while we converse. Bruno cheers, *"Brava, brava,"* at my efforts to speak Italian. His brown eyes glow under thick gray brows, a broad grin etches his leathery face, as we ramble through landscapes reminiscent of Renaissance paintings. I too am mesmerized by these majestic backdrops to daily life, as long as I occupy the passenger seat.

With Lucia driving, it's entirely different. She talks incessantly, and loudly, as if I were deaf. But in the process, my vocabulary is growing, as well as our friendship. Her dinner invitations are a five-star-event. I can still taste her pumpkin-stuffed ravioli and airy almond cake from days ago. Her auburn-streaked, short-cropped hair makes her appear younger than her fifty-seven years. Unlike Bruno, who addresses me as *Signora Pecki*, she treats me as a peer.

The day to pick up my rental car finally comes. The agency faxed me the contract two days ago. Without Lucia, I might never have faced this day. Looking back, I wish Bruno accompanied me, given his mild manner. Lucia, by comparison, has a way of adding sparks and drama to every situation. During the hour-long train ride to Florence, she imparts Italy's rules of the road. Her rushed recitation only increases my tension. By the time we arrive at Santa Maria Novella train station, my stomach is in knots.

At the car rental agency, I'm present in body, but a bundle of nerves. When the young woman at the desk hands me the car keys, I try to appear calm and capable. She guides us to the garage entrance and my fully automatic, four-door, navy blue Peugeot. Once behind the wheel, tension infiltrates every limb. When do I make my move, I wonder, gawking at the chaotic traffic soaring past. Despite a bombardment of cars, Lucia repeats, *"Vai, vai,"* go, go, overriding my caution, pushing me into a sea of suicidal drivers. As I slip into the nearest lane, she barks one command after another, in Italian. With my neck as stiff as steel, and choking from fumes, I pray the cars beside and behind us stay clear.

Until we reach Florence's perimeter, Lucia takes charge, flailing her arms, and screeching instructions: "Change lanes! Turn right! Merge here!" Between implementing her commands, deciphering signs to Siena, and dodging Vespas forging self-made lanes, my head is ready to crack.

When we reach a country road and I quit gasping, Lucia comments on the Peugeot's equipment. "There are not many autos like this here; they're for *pigri*, lazy, drivers," she says. So be it, I thought. Better lazy than maimed.

The next day, determined to navigate these dreaded local roads, I head to the nearby market. What should be a short ride turns into forty-five minutes of looping one way, then another, the market never in sight. I find myself in a labyrinth of dirt roads marked only by a cattle-crossing sign. But there's reason to smile when I gaze westward; a radiant tapestry of the sun's descent behind a medieval fortress, framed with towering cypresses. The words of the twentieth-century writer, Edith Wharton, come to mind: "picturesqueness is never far to seek when Italian masonry and Italian sunlight meet."

Even with a map in hand, I invariably get lost. While exploring the outskirts of Montalcino, renowned for its Brunello wine, Edith Wharton's words again ring true: "Italy is a land in which anything may happen, save the dull, the obvious, and the expected." I enter a road the width of an alley lined on both sides with cars. With nothing enthralling to see, I look for an exit. Oh nuts! I'm at a Dead End, at least ten feet above broad steps descending onto a piazza. No railing, no signs, no room to turn around. My heart thumps as loudly as windshield wipers on high. The only way out is to retrace the way in.

I quiver from head to toe maneuvering the car backwards,

uphill no less. After several deep breaths, I lightly tap the gas pedal, steering the car a foot at a time. Breathe, another foot, steady, steady. . . Oh no! A sharp left-hand turn, in reverse. My heart throbs against my throat. No way!

Clang, bang! The rear bumper hits the side of a car jutting beyond the yellow parking line. After calming myself from the immediate fright and resigning to an insurance hike, I feel forewarned: avoid unwise turns.

* * * * *

Unlike unwise turns, premature turns can bring new discoveries. After one such turn, I stumble upon a Roman amphitheater in Arezzo. Strolling the grounds of this ancient structure spurs my imagination— cheering crowds, men in togas, women draped in silk.

Another premature turn, this time outside the Renaissance town of Pienza, takes me to a pre-Christian church, with a carved fertility goddess gracing the entrance.

Subsequent turns pushed my driving skills up a notch, including launching me on the daunting Autostrada. During my first solo drive from Florence, despite following the directions to Rome via surface roads, I keep going in circles. With nightfall approaching, and an Autostrada sign for Rome popping into view, I grit my teeth and inch onto its lightning-speed lanes for the first time. I stay in the so-called "slow" lane, behind a caravan of large commercial trucks, as other motorists zip by.

An hour later, back home in one piece, I congratulate myself, and envision more routes for me to travel in my newly adopted world.

english major

by Chris Perry

i tried to imagine a twelve-sided model of
infinity, but i talked myself out of it. if you
can't divide by zero (i also tried that), then
you can't make a shape of infinity with
finite parts. you can decide what isn't but
not what is: that is decided for you. you
can say zero and you can say none but
you can't pretend they're the same thing.
yes is not love, heartburn is not love. also
not love: obsession, sex, eye-contact,
mutual fright, mutual obsession, noodles
(even really good noodles), saying "i love
you," saying "i want you, i only want you."
after experiments, too many to mention,
it seems love (and maybe infinity), is, in
fact, not twelve-sided, and not one-sided,
not even one-dimensional: a single point ---
love is exactly congruent with forgiveness.

Okasan's Avatar

by Momoyo Capanna

atop a round oak table
      inside a tall glass case
      stands a kimono-clad
      samurai doll

tucked inside
      her diamond-patterned obi
          stitched with sturdy strands
          of subtle grays and glistening gold
      drapes a double-edged sword

the samurai doll
      like a majestic crane
          stoic in her grace
          timeless vigilance
              stands alone
              in silent solitude

"So the writer who breeds more words than he needs, is making a chore for the reader who reads."

—*Dr. Seuss*

Sister

by Melinda Cohen

A death sentence.

That's what it felt like seven years ago when my younger sister, Jill, and her husband called to share that Jill had been diagnosed with Early Onset Alzheimer's. Jill was only 58 years old then. Suddenly, Life as I'd known it, flowing along with only the occasional small boulder in the stream to navigate around, seemed to hit an impassable cement wall.

Why Jill? My sweet, joyful sister who'd taught first grade, raised four active children, was a healthy, athletic person who could navigate a Black Diamond ski slope with ease, and send up a rooster-tail when waterskiing behind her family's boat. An accomplished baker, a creative maker of greeting cards, a loving friend who listened with an open heart and gently shared wise advice.

My best friend on Earth. The sibling I envisioned myself growing old with, sitting in our rocking chairs laughing over shared memories. How could this be happening to her?

Her caring husband and her now adult children formed a team of support and love, and explored all possible medications and treatments that might slow this insidious disease. My brother-in-law found a wonderful support group. He learned all he could about the best way to care for Jill, and himself, as he dealt with the slow but steady decline caused by Alzheimer's.

Now, seven years later, Jill is not the same person she used to be. She is still sweet, still smiles and can answer simple questions with a 'yes' or 'no.' Her devoted spouse and children make her a priority in their lives, include her in their outings, gently guide her on walks in their neighborhood.

At our family gatherings, we five siblings each find

time to sit and speak with Jill, hold her hand and show her recent photos on our phones. Although it's a one-sided conversation, she smiles and seems to enjoy being near us.

What felt like a death sentence for my beloved sister has instead created a situation where all the people she cared for and loved are now able to return that love to her. It still feels so unfair, so wrong, that Jill is slowly succumbing to this cruel disease. Yet in her own special way, Jill is still giving to all of us, providing us the opportunity to be accepting, to show we care, to offer our love and support.

While we probably won't end up together as elderly siblings in our rockers, she will always be my hero in so many ways.

On Seeing Monet's Nymphéas at the Biltmore Estate

by William Black

The lilies lie languid on the quiet pond
rose, butter and crimson crowns
resting in a watery tableau.
Through a fragile bridge of time
120 years long
they flow with a silent sorting of souls here
transfixed on benches, floor or standing unmoored
faces lifted, eyes lured,
a church of attention
for whom the world melts away.
Monet's hands composed his jardin d'eau
rerouted the Epte River
built the Japanese footbridge in the Clos Normand
and planted the new Latour-Marliac hybrids.
And now, a set of brushes, a mix of pigments, an artist's
aspiration
sweep from Giverny to Asheville
and embrace this translucent audience in their force.

Mindful Meditation
by Nola Neeley

When the mind settles
gently
into the heart
The soul slips
quietly
to the surface
The body rests
shoulders relax
breathing deepens

An inner feeling of peace
enwraps
my thirsting soul
A palpable sense of
soothing
comfort
Infuses every fiber
of my being
Inside and out

Oh, the joy and blessing
of quiet rest
and peace
Alone in the universe
just living
just being
I am born anew
Mind
Body
Spirit
       Becoming ME

Shake Those Boots

by Gordon Nicholson

I remember being seven and listening to every bit of advice my dad offered. Every time I visited Dad in the desert, a sharp warning was always aimed my way. I felt he could never be wrong about anything. I listened intently as his desert wisdom unfolded. How lucky I felt to be there with him, to share his life as we stood outside putting our boots on to work in an Upland lemon grove. "Watch out!" he shouted. "You don't know what'll crawl outta there. Shoes and boots left outside are perfect hiding places for varmints."

"What d'ya mean?" Holding my boot, I hesitated. "Varmints? They just bite the dust, don't they?"

"Okay, son, guess you haven't any idea what varmints are."

"Just bugs."

"More'n that. They're bad guys. Not like the cattle rustlers that Wyatt and Doc had to round up in Tombstone. These little varmints can really hurt a fella."

"Yeah?"

"Sure, some—like crickets, cockroaches, and spiders—just scare people. But scorpions are real bad. Out in the desert, there are lots of 'em, so better get in practice here now, and be on guard!"

Decades passed, but I never forgot his warning. As we stood outside his ranch house in southern Arizona, ready to stroll along a desert wash, I still braced for his familiar warning.

"Watch those tennis shoes!" he says. "You left 'em outside last night, boy. Shake 'em out good. "

I started to laugh, since I was no longer a boy and as tall as he by then.

"Not a joke," he said with a frown. "Here the varmints can gang up on you! The spiders are nasty. Tarantulas can scare the bejesus out of you! But you can have scorpion stings that send you rushing to the hospital. Worst of all, there are baby sidewinders that'll crawl into boots!"

"Wow! Dad, bet you never knew anyone who got bit."

"Oh, yeah? Let me tell you 'bout a ranch hand down in Nogales. He shook his boots and out fell a young Gila Monster. It woulda latched onto one of his toes and not let go till they cut its head off. The guy probably wouldn't have died, but it sure woulda made him sick for months."

Images of lurking Gila Monsters remained with me from childhood. I even looked up information on their habits. Each time I shook out my shoes, I always awaited some unpleasant surprise.

As usual, our hike went uneventfully that day, with little chatter. Even grown, I prized the time I spent learning from this naturalist, who had doubled as a part-time dad. I watched as he gazed at the empty desert, and then at clumps of Saguaros, some pale and withered. I wondered what he knew but had never shared with me. He once told me that storm clouds would form by noon from unseen moisture coming in from Mexico on the breeze, and he'd been right.

Now, every time I leave my shoes outdoors, I can still hear his warning. I pick up one shoe at a time, inverting it, shaking hard and then tapping it against a wall. At our condo in San Juan, years of practice finally bears fruit. As I mindlessly begin the routine outside the back slider, something jolts my senses. The first shoe goes through the familiar process I've done a hundred times before. Nothing comes out but air. Then, shaking the second shoe while trying to remember where my work gloves are located, something falls out and hits the patio floor. Yikes! Stunned, the varmint tries to turn over while my father's warning sends urgent distress signals to my brain. My bare foot could be in danger. A tarantula?

I hop backwards, my laser-like focus hoping it's not a Gila Monster just as it rights itself and slowly crawls off. Then a feeling of relief hits like desert rain. The creature I'd harbored is only a four-inch long, tail-less lizard. I laugh, recalling my dad's terse lessons from years ago.

Finally, after faithfully heeding the old sage's advice, it happens, not a deadly encounter, but an experience that makes me realize my dad had been right. Although his warning had been more meaningful in the desert, it's good to be cautious even in 'safe' South Orange County where the 'Age of Varmints' has passed—thanks to lawnmowers, weed whackers, blowers, pest control, and street sweepers—and my dad would get a kick out of the whole thing.

That evening I lift a wine glass in a toast, facing southeast. My mind spans 500 miles to Tubac, the final resting place of my departed mentor. He'd lived an intriguing life, in a very different time and place, and I've found joy in recalling these never-to-be-forgotten moments with him.

A Barefoot Evening

by John Perry

It's a barefoot evening.
Timid shadows hide
behind crimson Azaleas
and peek around
the front porch steps
of Elmira Johnson's
mustard-colored Victorian.
The house we call haunted
And only approach during daylight.

A gentle breeze
rustles dry, brown leaves
of the Sycamore trees
lining Main Street.
In nearby fields,
yellowing corn stalks rattle
and heads of barley
change from tan to gold
as they bow before
the last rays of sunlight
that stretch across the valley.

In the town square
blades of newly mown grass
feel warm and prickly
as my bare back presses
against the earth,
while my eyes keep watch
for the promised crescent moon
and my mind soars
toward emerging stars.

Tommy Preston torments my sister
with crawdads we brought back
from wading in the creek...
I bet they get married some day.
Lights go on in Tsuda's Grocery,
The Five & Dime, and The Corner Café.
When the streetlights come on
Mom calls us home for supper.
I've got to remember
to wash the summer off my feet
before I go inside.

"Get it down. Take chances. It may be bad, but it's the only way you can do anything really good."

—*William Faulkner*

dreams

by Sharon Voorhees

dreams
unfold
cards fall

align
with grounded
leaves

meant
to lay down
perfectly

Learning to Drive

by Sheila Roell

I stood at the kitchen table, rifling through the mail, hoping for something to add excitement to another monotonous hot summer day. A lone postcard stood out amongst the bills and sales flyers. I caught my name – Sheila Anne MacDonald printed in all capital letters across the front. I ignored the smaller print "to the parents of" above my name.

Flipping the card over, I read the paragraph; my eyes widened, and the need to giggle overcame me. I flipped back to see the return address, stamped on the upper left corner – "Midland Public School System, 101 Buttles Street, Midland, Michigan." I flipped the card again and read slowly

SHEILA ANNE MACDONALD

enrolled in Driver's Education

Beginning Wednesday, September 8, 1965

All classes held at Midland High School

Call TE-49607 with questions about placement.

I quickly removed the card from the stack of mail. I needed a plan before my parents learned about a class as crucial as Driver's Ed. Before the class started, I had to figure out how I could learn to drive without actually doing it. Driving was too important to learn in class. I needed to know a few basics beforehand. None of my friends had their licenses. I would be the first.

It was already August, and school started right after Labor Day. I didn't have any time to lose.

I was fifteen, and Driver's Ed would start in just a few days. My brother, Steve, had learned to drive the year before, but my uncle let him drive a bit on his land, and he got to drive the ski boat more than me plus, he drove my other uncle's tractor two or three times. He had skills. I didn't. I thought about my parents.

Mom: always agreed with whatever Dad said. She would not be a good teacher for me – way too excitable.

Dad would think I was too young. But he would help me. He might get cranky, but he would do it.

I approached Mom first, knowing she would direct me to Dad. Mom and I were shopping for school clothes the next day, and we had to bring my baby sister along. It wasn't ideal, but I didn't see a better time.

We had cokes at S.S. Kresge after shopping. My eight-year-old sister Shelley was acting out, and Mom was in a hurry but had promised her a treat if she behaved. It was now or never.

"So, Mom, we got a card from school that said I'm going to start Driver's Ed as soon as school starts, and I…"

"You're only fifteen. You're too young! You should wait a year."

"I'm not too young. I'll be sixteen before class ends. Everyone gets a license when they're sixteen. I don't think it can be changed anyway!"

"Talk to your father. He'll have to teach you a few things before you start. Where's the card? I never saw it."

"Oh, I have it. I thought it was addressed to me, but maybe it was addressed to you and Dad."

"Well, see what your father says"

I approached Dad that night.

"Dad, I'm supposed to learn to drive before I take Driver's Ed. When can we practice?"

"Well, not now. My dinner has to settle. Take the class, and then we'll see."

"But Dad, I only have …"

"Not now. I'm reading the paper. We can talk later."

Well, he didn't say no, I thought. I wanted to ask my brother, but he had football practice every night, so I figured that was an automatic no. Mom, who was in a good mood, smiled to herself. Why is she in such a good mood, I wondered. "

Mom made one of Dad's favorite dinners the next night, scalloped potatoes and meatloaf. After dinner, Dad slid his wallet into his back pocket and picked up the car keys.

"Sheila, let's go."

"Huh, where?"

"Driving. Let's get it done. I wanna get home."

Scrambling to the family's blue Ford sedan, I settled in the passenger's seat, butterflies in my stomach.

First, we went to the large parking lot of a local grocery store. We found an empty area as far away from the store as possible. There, Dad focused on showing me how to drive forward, backward, park, and check for traffic.

Finally, it was getting late when I asked to drive.

"Not now, not here. We'll go to a safer place."

With that, we headed off to the other side of town. A car pulled out as we pulled in through the beautiful gates that always stood open at The Midland County Cemetery.

Among all the dead people, I learned the basics on small one-way roads with small, short Stop signs on every corner and a traffic circle in the middle. After dark, in the family car, the radio turned off. I learned to back up a block at a time, parallel park, and angle park at the water stop.

Up and down the roads, we crawled. The speed limit was five mph. Sometimes we saw other students. We used our turn signals. I drove in the dark on clear nights and in the rain. My Dad remained critical, but we kept going to the cemetery.

Class started, and I was dismayed that the first six weeks consisted of classroom learning from books like "Michigan Rules of the Road" and "Driver's Safety and

Etiquette." Why didn't I know this? My brother laughed, making fun of me. It wasn't until the second six weeks that we were allowed on the driving range.

By then, Dad and I had put in plenty of cemetery time. I learned a lot and thought I was ready for a more robust driving experience. Dad was ready to turn me over to a qualified instructor.

We were asked to select a partner for the driving range work in class. I chose my friend Libby. She and I walked to the range with car keys attached to a #6 tag. Number six was the only car on the lot with a manual transmission. Dad had given me a few lessons in his car, a manual transmission but only a couple of times. I insisted Libby go first. After some fits and starts, Mr. Sheffield, our teacher, sauntered over.

"Trouble girls?" He gave us a quick lesson, and I immediately remembered the feel of a clutch. Libby struggled but caught on quickly. Disaster averted, we completed the six weeks, did the road work, and received our certificates to take the actual driver's test at the police station. I had turned sixteen five weeks earlier.

My actual driver's test was on a manual transmission car, where I had to parallel park on a very steep hill on a rainy day. I was nervous but thankful I had driven a manual in school. If luck has ever been on my side, it was on my side that day. The officer was even impressed. I passed the test and had my temporary license.

I promptly drove my mother to my grandmother's and, very precisely, but accidentally parked with two wheels up on the curb.

You see, The Midland County Cemetery didn't have curbs.

"Always be a poet, even in prose."

—*Charles Baudelaire*

Rhythm and Blues

by Olivia Starace

SATURDAY
music from an old radio
small shoes atop her father's shoes
Look Yolanda he shouts to the mother
This girl's got   rhythm
                    pictures tomorrow
                    of you and your sisters
                    the father said placing the camera
                    on a high shelf

the girl curiously gazed
at that camera on high
not letting time pass by...

SUNDAY
Four girls dressed for Sunday Mass
Sitting like little princesses on the grass
Four girls calm not shaken
Waiting for pictures to be taken

Father marching in agitated flutter
Who pressed down the camera shutter
He shouted spitting profanity
In a split moment's insanity

It was the one wearing frilly white socks
The one who twirled her fingers through her curly locks
The one singing her audacious melody
IT WASN'T ME
He gave her a wallop
Then sat her back down
These words for follow-up
SMILE   NO FROWNS

She thought to her angry self
She would not smile
She DID NOT smile
What shows is her pouting profile

From that mad wallop
This was the follow-up
Dancing atop her father's shoes   GONE
She had no rhythm from that day   ON

Proving the words from an old song
'Guilty Feet Have Got No Rhythm'

Inspired by: "CARELESS WHISPER"
By George Michael, co-written by bandmate
Andrew Ridgeley 1981, released July 24, 1984

The Inner Critic

by Nancy Pfaffl

Where is the origin of the inner critic?
Is it delivered with each new baby?
Tucked in tightly under the umbilical cord?
Sent home from the hospital strapped with the infant into
    the car seat?

Does it grow and develop inside, squeezing in under the heart?
Popping through the surface, like a new tooth in a toddler?
Or the chickenpox bursting out from under the skin?
Does it emerge with speech when we learn what "no" and
    "bad" mean?

Does a first grader absorb it at school,
    when someone says the picture drawn is dumb or
    the spelling wrong?
By high school has the inner critic made itself at home,
    Firmly entrenched for life?

How much has the inner critic grown by college age?
Does it now boss the young adult around?
Dominating decisions and calling the shots?
Holding back playfulness, trying new things?

Is the inner critic in charge of adulthood,
Draining confidence away like melting snow,
Sanding away self-worth into powdery dust
Until all that remains is a wet sandy mess.
Or...can the inner critic be washed away
    with a warm shower and plenty of soap?

Can the inner critic be excised like a surgical wound,
    muzzled like a dangerous beast?
Left behind at the train station when the train departs,
Sent away on a spaceship to a distant galaxy.

Can the inner critic's power be harnessed?
Could it be tempered with fusion into something more useful?
Could it sound the alarm when we need to pay attention?
Could it help to correct our course,
Adjust our attitude, guide us to firmer ground?
Might it become an ally, who will tell us the absolute truth?
A mentor, who can teach us to become our bravest self?

The Grandfather Clock
by Mark Van Houten

Elevated on the tips of her tiny toes Rachel's probing eyes could barely peer over the window's ledge to survey the gloomy streets below. Immersed in darkness, a lonely lamplight cast a cone of illumination over animated men searching for Jews. With rifles hoisted over their shoulders, the men boldly displayed swastikas on their military hats and jackets.

Rachel's mother, Chaika, broke the silence with an urgent message. "Come away from the window, Rachel, so they don't see you. We don't want to attract their attention." Her mother beckoned by the wave of her hand to join her at the Shabbos table in the shadows at the center of the living room.

Rachel, squinting, hand walked her way through the darkened apartment, inching around the aged, deep-buttoned Chesterfield, and creeping over the musty Persian throw rug, muted in deep purples and green. For guidance she ran her fingertips along the faded wallpaper in floral design, selected by her parents for its rhythmic balance, order and harmony. Photographs of family, framed in tasteful display, clung to the wallpaper for support. As she edged across the drafty fireplace, her saddened gaze ascended along the tall, hand-engraved, mahogany box, positioned as a majestic sentinel, upon which was perched the face of the silent grandfather clock, seeming to oversee Shabbos from above.

"Come help me light the candles to welcome in the Sabbath," implored Menachem, who gently spread over his shoulders his lovingly adorned tallit, which displayed bright Biblical scenes of ancient Jewish worship. He stroked the thick waves of his greying beard and adjusted his yarmulke over his balding head. Curls of dangling hair strands cascaded over both ears.

"We must fulfill our part of the Covenant to worship God, so God will hear us, and take good care of us," explained her father. In Rachel's imagination the austere face of her grandfather was engraved in the wooden casing of the clock face, which seemed to approve with a loving nod.

To begin the service, her mother, cloaked in a dark, modest dress, laid the embroidered cloth over the challah. She ignited the candles that accompanied the ritual wine glasses on the sacred table. Chanting softly, she first closed then covered her eyes with the cup of her palms, momentarily hiding from view the family's dire circumstances. Her father chanted softly into God's ear, so as not to be heard by soldiers in the street, and likely those in their building, as well.

Rachel's father spoke. "Barukh ata adonai Eloheinu. Blessed art thou, oh Lord our God, who is trustworthy in His covenant to fulfill His sacred promise to shield and protect His people, Israel. With a mighty hand God will rescue the people of Israel from their travails, as is our Lord's solemn promise to his people, while enslaved in Egypt."

"Watch over us," thought Rachel, who then studied the face of the silent grandfather's clock, hugging the fireplace mantle. The hands of the clock, pointing up at 10 and 2, appeared to her like her father's arms unfolded and reaching to the heavens in prayer.

"I wish grandfather could be with us tonight," whispered Rachel, interrupting the prayers. Chaika explained with gentle directness, "Grandfather Yitzhak's clock stopped ticking on the day he was taken by the soldiers, as if the clock knew that grandfather had passed in their hands. Our deepest wish is for this lovely clock to welcome grandfather's spirit to return and live quietly among us always."

Her mother was about to remove the linen covering the challah, when loud knocking reverberated through the door and throughout the apartment.

"Achtung!" bellowed the soldier's voice. "Wer ist da?" Recognizing the impending peril, Rachel and her parents scrambled for cover.

"Mach sofort die fur auf!" Within the moment two husky SS officers crashed the door open with a mighty fist, and surveyed the apartment lit only by two Shabbos candles.

"Sind Sie auch Judisch? Hander hoch. Juden verboten und infiziert ungeziefer!" Rachel's parents scurried behind the pantry curtain, dragging Rachel in tow. "Rachel," Chaika insisted. "Hitler told the soldiers that Jews were vermin to be exterminated. Our lives are in danger should the soldiers find us. So, hush!"

"I will pray for grandfather's protection," thought Rachel.

The thunderous rumble of a passing tank shook violently the apartment building to its foundation. With that, the grandfather clock revived to 'bong, bong'; then commenced to 'tick, tock, tick, tock'. Rachel's eyes shown radiantly. She turned in amazement to her parents. "Momma, Momma." Rachel spoke above a whisper. "I hear it. tick, tock, tick, tock. The clock is saying 'Yitzhak, Yitzhak'. Do you hear it?" Rachel's voice now rose in volume. "Grandfather is reaching out to us. I must go to the clock for his protection."

"Quiet, Rachel," implored Chaika. "We must remain silent and not attract the soldiers."

"No. Momma," Rachel pleaded. "The grandfather clock is calling to us. He wants me to go to him." Rachel loosened her mother's grip, and barreled on all fours through the apartment, reaching out fearlessly to the voice of her grandfather.

The heads of the soldiers turned to the muffled rumble of Rachel scurrying across the Persian rug to reach the loudly animated grandfather clock. Catching a fleeting glimpse of her, one of the soldiers shouted, "Wer da? Handenen hoch." After a moment of silence, the soldiers let loose a blinding hail of bullets that tore through the sofa, releasing feathers and fragments of wood chips into a cloud of gunfire smoke. The butt end of their rifles slashed across the sacred table, smashing the Kiddush glasses, and spewing the red wine like blood onto the Persian rug.

Chaika and Menachem huddled silently, praying that Rachel would emerge from the darkness. Yet, she was silent, even after the soldiers left. The ticking of the grandfather clock had also gone silent. Rachel's breathless parents stared silently into the darkness of their apartment.

Gazing from the broken Shabbos candles and across the silent apartment and through the window looking outward and downward, they saw the gloomy street below was silent. All the streets of the city were silent. The countryside extending from the city to the sea was silent.

All the earth was silent. All the celestial candles, as stars in the sky and a trillion galaxies beyond, as far as all humanity knew, were silent. The entire universe in its totality from the beginning of time remained silent.

A Sorrow Comes

by Nola Neeley

A sorrow comes, a trial deep,
A burden you can't bear
To shoulder all alone, I know -
I know, for I've been there.

You feel like curling in a ball
and rocking quietly
While streaming tears inside your soul
are falling — endlessly.

Where can you turn?
How can you find the road or path beyond?
You must reach in, and out, and up
For help to make you strong.

Reach in, inside yourself
in times of loss and grief
There's power hidden deep inside
Reach in to find relief.

Reach out to friends and loved ones dear
Whose hearts are aching too.
With gentle words encircle them
Reach out, they'll comfort you.

Reach up to heaven and gentle peace
will fall like sparkling rain
To wash away your grief and tears
and make you whole again.

By reaching, in, and out and up
you'll feel your heart entwined
With knowledge, faith and solace sweet -
Your precious soul refined.

"You can make anything by writing."

— C.S. Lewis

I'll Cry with You

by Nola Neeley

My heart, it seems, begins to mend
the aching's less severe
The heartache and the memories dim,
my eyes refuse to tear.

For deep inside my heart is raw
and no one else can know
The healing's on the outside
Inside, I'm hurting so,

The tears are falling in my soul
When will this longing end?
And then come words, so sweet and low
I'll cry with you, my friend

I'll cry with you, I'll ease your hurt,
I'll wipe your tears away
For as my Son, in agony,
Hung on the cross that day

You cried with me, from heaven's veil
Your tender heart pierced too,
Now I feel your grief and pain
And I will cry with you.

I'll ache with you until you're strong
I'll feel the pain you feel
Until the blessing from my Son
Can sweetly, softly heal.

Journal Entry

by Momoyo Capanna

Monday, June 6, 2022
7:45 AM

Good morning, Love. Yesterday, after church service and coffee hour, the kids decide on Jersey Mike's for lunch. As I walk to the car, Sam, who just turned 11, comes running after me.

"Grandma, can I ride with you? Dad said I could."

"Sure, come on."

He scurries into the passenger seat and looks at me for approval. I nod and give him an okay. I'm guessing that's not his usual place in the family SUV.

"Well, what have you been up to?" I ask.

"I'm writing a story about Mace Windu."

"Who's that?"

"He's a Jedi Master of Star Wars."

"Ooo kay..." Well, Sam lost me there.

"That's great. I'm glad you're writing. Grandpa John loved to write. In fact, you and Grandpa John have a lot in common. You both like to write, enjoy playing the drums, and love pizza. And, you're a Capanna. That's Italian, you know."

"Yes, I'm half Italian... and part English and Japanese."

I am stunned.

John, I remember when our first grandson was born, you said to me, "You are now Grandma Momoyo, just Grandma Momoyo." I knew what you meant. I was a grandmother and not a step-grandmother.

I turn to Sam, smile, and say, "Yes, you are. You are Italian, English, and Japanese."

Thank you, John. I love you. I miss you.

Penelope's Pencil Pouch

by Nicole Sandoval Gurgone

Looking in my pencil pouch
Through my artist eyes
Everything looks so different to me
My pencil, scissors, and eraser
are all staring right back at me
Showing a different image ready to be used by me
My pencil is long and sharp
Standing to attention
Listening to each word
So it can jot it down for me
Words quickly appear
down on the paper in front of me
Stories poems, oh, just about anything you would like to know
Then lying down on the side of me
Is a pink soft rectangular shape
That can erase almost anything
Once there, now gone
Its like those words never meant anything at all
Erased from my page
Only the things I truly want to say
Will be seen and printed
for all my teachers and friends
to read and praise
But wait
I see two big oval eyes looking over at me
Legs sharp and shiny
What can you be
A trim here
A cut there
Need to use with special care

It's my scissors
That can shape my paper
Any which way
How I want it cut to fit my story book page
My pouch is a tool case
Waiting for directions from me
All to create words on paper for all to read

"You have to write the book that wants to be written. And if the book will be too difficult for grown-ups, then you write it for children."

—Madeleine L'Engle

Aunt Patsy
by Margaret de Jaham

I called her Auntie Mame
She laughed with gusto
And made you feel appreciated.

Her poetry reflected the eye of an artist
Her art was poetic, lyrical
Her images evoked a beautiful soul

She found humor in daily happenings
And recounted them with flair
Always lifting our spirits

Due to arthritis, she could no longer paint
Until she strapped brushes to her wrists
If Renoir could do it, so could she

The world still needs her kind
So full of joy and wonder
And so do I

I miss my Auntie Mame.

Dead Man Gazes

by John Henning

Hiding in the livery barn, Joe leaned against a side wall and peered through a knothole. Wagon wheel ruts marred the broad cross street between the barn and General Store. Three open oblong crates leaned upright against the store's sidewall.

Each narrow rough-hewn plank box framed a fresh dead Lawson brother. Their crates grouped together, they posed in natural stances. Wes, Leroy, and Matt each stared with a dead man's gaze.

"I was on the way, boys," Joe muttered. "Got delayed avoiding a posse." A sigh greeted sadness. "What happened?"

The brothers' silent gazes heightened the unknown.

Joe changed his angle of view. Several paces left, a parked Undertaker's wagon held a stack of crate lids. An empty oblong crate hung out of the wagon.

Sunrise glowed over the wagon's two mules, stretched down the street, and chased shadows out of ruts. Morning sunbeams streamed over a sturdy tripod and large camera. This rising angle of light deepened details.

A photographer stood behind the camera. Through the lens, he studied the cropping of the inert subjects. Portrait in focus, he stepped aside and waited for a brief, more desirable range of light. Voices disrupted his concentration. He glanced away.

Again, Joe changed his angle of view. To the right, four men stood outside the camera frame. The town Sheriff and Undertaker faced two cowboys with backs to the barn. Gathering in breath, Joe put an ear to the knothole. Except for random outbursts, the four men droned in murmurs.

In a huff, Joe pushed away from the rough wall. Clenched eyelids squeezed his sight. He tried to rub out smoldering fatigue. Trail weary, what he now witnessed didn't make sense. He leaned back against the wall and peeked through the knothole. Stronger daylight sharpened the tight scene. The two cowboys shifted away from stabbing sunlight, exposing familiar features.

"Son of a bitch," Joe whispered. "Chugg McNurt and Runt Tathers. You no good, self-proclaimed cousins." He watched them shake hands with the Sheriff and gesture toward the Lawson brothers. "Dirty rat bastards, what have you done?"

A burst of coarse laughter slashed Joe's uncertainty. Shock of their betrayal enraged his senses. Hatred burned in his throat.

He stepped backward with clenched fists. His leathery tongue dabbed his cracked mouth corners. A consuming void within him, carved by days on the run, now festered with vengeance. Parched taste buds, dry as the stable dust swirling around his boots, ached to savor revenge.

Again, Joe squinted through the knothole. The daylight now produced desirable contrasts. Having timed an exposure, the photographer capped the lens. In a swift process, he changed plates and exposed film. He repeated the routine and then paused.

"Hey," called out Chugg, "How 'bout a picture of me and Runt on either side?"

"Cost ya," the photographer replied.

"Well, we're good for it. You can ask the sheriff," Runt boasted.

Sheriff nodded, "They're good for it," he vouched.

"Aw-right," the photographer agreed, "get over there

quick, but don't kick up the dust."

The cowboys scampered to either side of the crates.

Guns drawn, Chugg waved his gun barrel at the brothers' corpses. "Don't any of you move and ruin our picture."

Runt laughed, "They can't move, you fool."

They posed with guns pointed at the brothers. Chugg sneered with a farcical expression. Runt surrendered to an uneven silly grin. "OK, boys, photo be ready tomorrow."

The cousins holstered their guns. "Won't be seein' you guys anymore," taunted Runt.

"And they thought they was too good for us," Chugg added.

As they walked away, Leroy's eyes seemed to follow them.

Bolstered by posing, Chugg blurted out, "Ya know, sheriff, with your sealed letter and that photo, we should have no problem claiming this territory's reward."

"Stop by my office later today." A soft flatness in his tone. "Say, after 4 o'clock."

"Hey, sheriff," the undertaker called out, "We need to nail down lids and move along. But someone stole my hammer and nails."

"What type of town you runnin', sheriff?" Chugg needled the lawman.

Sheriff squinted one eye, tilted his head that way, "Why don't you see if there's hammer and nails in the livery barn."

Chugg pointed and ordered, "Runt, go check the barn."

Uncertain, Runt looked at the sheriff, then at the undertaker, then at Chugg. He turned and stared at the barn's sidewall. With reluctant steps, he started toward Main Street.

Joe hadn't heard everything, but gestures and reactions

filled in the gaps. He jumped away from the wall. Frantic cold pulses flushed through him, adding to his existing aches. Hidden, now trapped, he sparred with desperation to survive. "Keep a clear mind," he coaxed himself.

On the street, Chugg yelled out, "Hurry up, Runt. Flies'll be gathering. They gotta get these boot hill bunks covered in dirt linens."

A grimace creased the sheriff's face. "Holdup, Runt," he ordered, "C'mon back."

"What now, sheriff?" Chugg challenged.

Sheriff turned to the Undertaker. "Go to the General Store. They have a load of hammers and nails. Tell 'em the sheriff's office will pay for the hammer if they donate the nails."

Runt returned and stood next to Chugg.

The sheriff continued. "I'd appreciate you giving us a hand with unloading the wagon, nailing the lids, and burying."

"Hell, Sheriff," Chugg protested, "we helped you kill 'em. That oughta be enough."

"As I recall, you fingered 'em but didn't pull any triggers." The sheriff's face tightened, "Now, you need a sealed letter; you need to give us a hand."

Drawn back to the knothole by the sheriff's call to Runt, Joe saw his situation change. Two cowboys walked to the wagon and started unloading crate lids. The undertaker returned with a hammer and bag of nails. Joe jumped away from the wall and scurried to saddle his horse. When finished, he checked the cross street.

There appeared to be a brief chance of escape. He led his horse onto Main Street and turned away from the General

Store. After a few tentative steps, he mounted the horse. As he settled in the saddle, apprehension tightened his skin and thinned his breath. Leaning forward against an urge to look back, he rode out of town in a casual gait.

Uneven and narrow, the dirt route wavered alongside railroad tracks. A few hours riding induced Joe to halt and dismount. Starving, dehydrated, dirty, and incensed, he leaned against his horse. The animal kept him upright.

His chin rested on a collarbone. Shaded by his hat brim, he took a final look back. But the terrain obscured the town, just as unresolved circumstances obstructed thoughts. The horse stepped forward. Joe strained to crawl into the saddle, then urged his mount onward.

An hour later, they crossed the territorial line. Sometimes the difference between a respectable citizen and an outlaw depended upon powers behind public opinion, territorial lawmen, and presiding judges.

Joe clung to his horse for another hour. Late afternoon, the road merged with another Main Street. The horse bobbed its head and stuttered.

Over the next few days, Joe ate, drank, and took comfort. All revived him. But nothing sated a primary need of atonement for his brothers' dead man gazes.

Good Morning, Baba

by Ghaffar Pourazar

How are you today?
Does he remember me?
I hold his hand; he responds
by holding mine. He's in a good mood.
It begins.
I escort him to the bath,
turn on the bright light.
Will you wash your face?
Do you have a wee-wee or not?

Dad, don't do that with your hands
He has bad habits in the bathroom,
cannot find the water stream, touches
things like a blind man, feels the water
with his hand. Ah and Ha combine into Ah-Ha.
He brightens, wets his fingers.
Baba, wash both hands. He refuses.
I push his left elbow. He resists.
Then he feels the hot water, it pleases.

He scoops his right hand like a bowl
and pours water to the left.
Once his hands are together
he washes them both with pleasure.
Wash your face. He doesn't listen.
I wet my hand and rub his face.
He pulls back at first. I insist.
Remember? This is washing face.
He turns around to leave.
Close the tap, Baba.

He turns off the cold tap.
That was great, no, don't touch that.
Now he's opened the hot tap.
Close it…yes…Baba…no leave it…not again.
Oh, you opened it…well, whatever.
I'm amused but disappointed.
I hear a loud "thhoooofffgh" as he
Blows his nose with a horrible sound.

Okay, Baba, now dry your hands.
He reaches for the paper stand.
He dries the top, he dries the bottom,
Hands together, he hums with pleasure

I pull him up to sit, pull him up to stand
and walk him to the door.
It's not yet seven am.

Goodnight, Baba

by Ghaffar Pourazar

Dad, why are you so grumpy,
why do you look so tired?
You slept all night,
for nearly 12 hours.

Dad, look at the sky, look at
the flowers, listen to the birds,
look at those tall trees.
You still wanna lie down?

Okay, you can lie down,
but don't worry, everything
is fine. Everyone is well,
everything is taken care of.

Sleep well, go into the world,
you prefer to be in. The lovely memories
the horrible memories, I'm not sure
anymore, which you prefer.

You can easily go to either,
as if it doesn't matter,
as if you're out of control, as if
you can't tell the difference,

You actually like them both,
you prefer them to the present,
but it becomes anti-Tao,
not wanting to be in the present.
all the poems ever written,

all the artists who found their moment,
in the presence of NOW, and you
want to get out? You resist, you deplore.

You kick and punch to escape
a gentle night. After telling him all is well,
I wonder if I believe it.
Good night, Baba. Good night.

"Tears are words that need to be written."

—*Paulo Coelho*

A Single Red Rose

by Lee Milton

He stands in the crowded reception area at the Tom Bradley International Terminal at LAX, holding a single red rose, feeling like a fool. Dressed in khakis, boat shoes without socks, a robin's egg blue Tommy Bahama linen shirt, classic southern California attire, he doubts this moment and everything about himself. What the hell was he doing here? What was he thinking?

It'd been three years since his wife blindsided him, walking out, grinning ear to ear, as she shed him like a snake it's skin, catching him by surprise, stunning him speechless. Except to ask repeatedly, "Why, why?"

"Going my separate way, can't do this anymore," her explanation as she pulled down the driveway in her fully packed, twelve-year-old Toyota Avalon. "I'll be back for the rest of my things."

The house bought for the two of them now echoed hollow, her office vacant, the door closed to hold in the memories, visions of her sitting at her desk, barefoot, earnestly conducting business, her sight, and fragrance. Coming home to silence, the 65" flat screen turned on for companionship and background noise to keep the quietude at arm's length. The formerly bright and colorful house was sullen and dour, less his safety and joy, now a stultifying prison.

The pain diminished at a glacial pace, contrasted with previous personal breakups, all of which could be categorized "What was her name again?" Postmortem, he discovered the depth of his love for her, measured by the length of time he mourned losing her, etched on his soul.

"What the hell's wrong with me?" he asked his therapist. "Why is it taking so long to be free of her?"

"You loved deeply for the first time," she explained. "Love lost can be excruciating." His morning mantra, as he stared bleary-eyed in the mirror, his hair part of some Halloween fright mask, became unprintable for polite society.

Time ticked by; he traveled his eleven-state region, attended trade shows, dated, but felt alone, even in the occasional afterglow of rare boom-boom happy endings. A friend suggested porn, and he opened this door, only to discover a vast world of sexual perversion and adventure unimagined. He was stunned to see the varieties and degradations people made public, even recognized a couple acquaintances. He stumbled into the world of international women wanting to come to America, not just for shopping malls and glamour, but the men. It was a revelation.

He clicked on a site of European ladies searching for western (European or, better yet, American) men. Drop dead gorgeous women, stunning, hungry to come to the freedoms of a new, exciting land of opportunity, and men who weren't alcoholics and abusive.

A brief query led to a longer one, followed by photos and longer emails, often alluring and sensual, and emotional pleas for how to make a meeting happen. The photos were tantalizing, with their come hither stares and curious English phrasings. Still, there were the warnings about scams and come ons used by these beauties as bait to separate a naïve American man from his dollars. There were also stories from delirious, ecstatic guys with their new mates whose main goal seemed to be making their man happy. What to believe?

Real life truth or dare, with tangible consequences, or "Ya pays yer money and takes yer chances." Was he communicating with a possible dream girl, whose imputed inner beauty matched the gorgeous femme fatale photo, or some hairy, sweaty beast tapping outcome on missives to scam money?

"I need $1,853 for plane fare," came a request on the sixth post, after a pronouncement of love, along with a steamy photo and implied promise of so much more. Love after a few emails and photos? Where's the emotional stability in this? Of course, emotional stability and love are too often oxymorons, oil and water. "Flight info to follow."

He hit SEND for the credit card payment, unsure of his status as either a moron or a lucky pilgrim. It's only money, easy come, easier go. If it's a naïve, outright stupid setup, he'll replace it next week in some other closed deal. What the hell.

Here he stands, lost in the crowd. It's a Chamber of Commerce weather day, sunny, warm, a gentle breeze with a hint of salty air, the full array of southern California colors on display to welcome guests. He looks around, self-conscious, thinking this display of himself, so obvious and cheesy, some lone guy, standing around on one foot and another, holding a single red rose, scanning the crowd for the right face. He notices two other guys, one younger and one much older, holding a single red rose, acting much the same as he.

Scanning the deplaning crowd, hoping to spot her, he sees one of the red rose carriers greet his traveler and watches their awkward meeting. Head nods, handshakes, tenuous hugs, that first meeting where both parties ask themselves, "What the hell am I doing here, and is this really her/him?" Elation, disappointment, compromise. Fantasy collides with reality.

Hanging tough, he searches the incoming crowd, hoping to see his beautiful Ukrainian princess, gold-brown, shoulder-length hair, green eyes, trim, with great...

"Excuse me," comes a voice to his left, broken English. "Are you Joshua?" He turns, and there she is. "I am Iliana, from Odessa. I have not met Joshua Howard yet. You have red rose. Are you him or someone else?"

Stunned, speechless, not so much by her actual presence as her beauty, he stammers, "Uh, yeah, I'm, a, Josh." He hands her the rose. She blushes, and they both smile.

"I am here for you." She reaches out her hand, and he takes it; to shake, to hold. Her shy smile dazzles, framing near-perfect white teeth. "I'm hungry, not eaten for twelve hours since leaving home. Can we eat?" He continues staring, not responding. "Did I say wrong? I'm sorry, but . . ."

"Lunch coming up; great American food. We can do Mexican or Chinese, or . . . I know. In-N-Out Burger." Perfect.

Janie

by Karen Ward

The telephone rang.

"Hello!"

"Um . . .um. I . . . ah. . . ." I recognized the soft, halting voice of my friend and classmate, Kathy Conway. It was a Sunday morning in 1958, and I was ten years old.

"My mother. . . ah . . wants-to-talk-with-your-mother!" she said.

"Okay, just a minute."

I wondered what was up.

I placed the receiver on the small telephone table we kept by the dining room window. My mother was at late mass, so I called my father, who was in the kitchen preparing vegetables for Sunday dinner.

"Mrs. Conway wants to talk to Mummy," I said.

My father quickly appeared in the doorway. Wiping his hands with a dish towel, he made his way around the dining table, picked up the telephone, and said hello.
He remained silent for a few minutes.

Then, speaking softly, he said, "Yes. Yes. I understand. I appreciate your telling us." Then he hung up and turned to me. Why did he look so serious?

Karen, I have something to tell you … "

"What is it?" I asked. "What happened?"

"It's about Janie, Janie Benedetto," he said. "She had been sick."

I knew that. She'd had a cold. She'd missed some school, but now it was school vacation, so that's why I hadn't seen her.

"She had to go to the hospital," he said. "They had to do an operation. . . . and. . .. .she died."

What? What? Died?

Died. Janie had died.

He said that she had Cancer.

Cancer? No. That made no sense.

"She died in surgery," he said. "There was nothing they could do."

What?

I didn't know what to do. How do I act? What was my body supposed to do? It didn't know what to do with itself! My mind was a jumble. I knew about death, didn't I? I wasn't a baby. My Great Aunt Min had died, and I went to her wake, but she was in her 80's, and I didn't know her very well.

Janie was ten.

My thoughts ran together. Janie. My friend. Hadn't I just gone to her birthday party where she wore a blue and white checked suit? She liked me! I wasn't her best friend; Kathy Conway was that. But I had often been lonely and was so happy she was my friend.

Janie and I both lived on Preston Street in Wakefield, Massachusetts, I in an old gray shingled farmhouse, and she in a more important pink stucco house up the street. We sat beside each other in Mrs. Luther's fifth-grade class at Montrose School. She was a little girl. Like me! And she was dead?

Dead.

As my father spoke, confusion flooded my mind and a chill overtook my body. I was a kid, and my friend was dead.

I remember wandering into the small room just off the dining room. I sat down at the piano and played. What did I play? I don't remember. I was usually such a talker, but now I was silent. I just kept playing the piano.

After a while, my mother came home from church. What did she say? I don't remember. Did she hug me? I don't know. Maybe she did. Did I cry?

Why don't I remember? I remember Kathy Conway calling. And the news that Janie was dead. And the piano. I remember the piano. It was my comfort, my escape. I couldn't talk to my parents. Or maybe I didn't know what to say. I felt embarrassed! So awkward. And they couldn't talk to me or didn't know how to talk to me. There was no lesson to be taught. No moral to this story. So, what was there to say?

My mother was a practical person, yet she was often emotional, crying over one thing or another. But those were her emotions, her wounds. She was not comfortable with other people's emotions. And certainly not with a child's sadness. Not that.

But she did get the information: there would be a wake at a funeral home near the Square in Wakefield and later a private family funeral.

Two days later, on Tuesday evening, my mother took me, my sister Pam, and my brother Jack to the wake. The youngest of us, Jimmy, did not come, as he was too little.

After parking the car, we walked down the concrete path and up the steps into the front room of an older and sprawling white clapboard house that was now MacDonald's Funeral Home. We signed a book and were shown into a room to the right where lots of people were standing in a line. The scent of a summertime rose garden filled the room, but this was no garden. There were red, white, and yellow roses, but they poked not from the ground but from stiff glass and metal vases scattered throughout the room, their stems cut, their soil missing. Quiet sniffles and low voices penetrated the silence as people moved through the line to greet Janie's family.

Then I saw her! Janie! Lying in a casket encased in pink. Bridged by wide-cut bangs, her short, dark hair lay upon a pink satin pillow, framing the familiar but now lifeless face of a child.   Closed eyelids hid what I knew were brown eyes.

Was that really Janie?

Yes.

It was Janie.

And she was dead.

Forever.

Suddenly, I could not stop crying. My sister and brother were crying, too. We each knelt at the casket to pray for a moment, and then it was time to go. As I walked to the car, still sobbing, my mother said, "I wouldn't have brought you to the wake if I knew it would upset you so much."

Did she hold me in her arms and let me cry?

No.

She took us home.

After that, we just went on with life. There were no therapists, no social workers, no exploring feelings. Maybe a prayer now and then. And the dreaded word Cancer was never spoken.

So, I went pretty silent about Janie.

I returned to school. For the rest of the year, Mrs. Luther left Janie's desk empty, I suppose to honor her.

But it was the desk right next to mine! I felt her absence every day. For a time after Janie's death, I would sometimes go over to Janie's house in the afternoon to play school with her younger sister Georgia. Her mother welcomed me, even though I was a lot older than Georgia. Maybe she understood why I came even if I did not.

Up the street from my house and not far from Janie's house, there was a squat white building called the Crystal Community Club. Behind it hid a tiny skating pond surrounded by a footpath. That path became my secret place. For a long time after Janie died, when the weather was warm, usually in the late afternoon, I would go there alone.

Singing softly to myself, I walked around and around and around the pond. I never told anyone I did that.

Those singing walks marked the beginning of my reflection about life. It was 1958, and I was ten years old.

At the
Water's Edge

by MJ West

A young couple
with three little girls
spreads a blanket, chairs,
buckets and toys on the beach.

The children's father
sinks a fringed pink umbrella
deep into the sand;
their mother opens a basket
filled with snacks and drinks,
then rubs sunscreen over
the girls' tender bodies.

At the water's edge,
holding their children's hands,
they lift them high in the air
and swing their toes
across the soft, foamy surf.

Watching this scene
is a step back into
my own past, remembering
love and happiness
in the summer light.

Summers are fleeting by,
but it doesn't matter what
has come before or
what's beyond the horizon,

I'm still here,
in the moment,
lingering at the water's edge,
feeling how lucky I am.

"Words are a lens to focus one's mind."

—Ayn Rand

Deep Dreams

by Olivia Starace

take me again to the edge of the universe
out in the joyous   quiet   diamond   edgeless sky
where I sat at your knee while you turned the pages
of wisdom   filling me
                filling me
with each softened stroke of your hand
on my head
                              you taught me

these words unspoken   soaked in joy
take me
I thirst for the gift of the wise
take me again
to where the stars cascade
into a rush of light
filling me
                Filling Me

Filling
        ME
with the wisdom
there   at the quiet   diamond   edgeless sky

Read the Signs

by Deberah Porter

Heather lives above the Chinese laundry. When she saw the For Rent sign, she knew it was a sign. Steam from below hangs in front of the apartment window like a sheer, cumulous cloud.

Can she turn this free steam into a unique operation? She has an idea…time to test her theory.

Then bang…a terrible car crash below. The shaken driver tells the officer, "Up there, I saw a green-faced, Turban-wrapped head with cucumber slices for eyes hanging in the mist above the laundry." The police took him away for drunk driving.

With Heather's Facial Spa dreams dashed, again she looks for a sign. Then while window shopping, she sees it. A sign that read… "If you're Looking for a Sign, this is it."

Autumn

by Sharon Voorhees

Time for sadness
after love that died
in the faded sun.

Time for solitude
to answer questions
summer carried.

Time to write unfinished poems
and sing untitled songs
before winter freezes them forever.

Time to end
and begin again.

Morning After the Rain

by John Perry

The rain must have come and gone
early this morning.
It had to be after midnight
because I didn't hear raindrops
dancing on the shingles
before I fell asleep.

And when I awoke
there was only the tap... tap... tap
of occasional drops
sliding from the eaves
and the broad leaves of the Sycamore
outside the bedroom window.

Runoff puddles the pansy beds,
bows the heads of lilacs
that perfume the front steps.
It chases fat earthworms onto the sidewalk
where the neighbor's cat
paws them into twitchy wiggles.

Sunlight slips across the boulevard,
climbs the backs
of wine-colored Crepe Myrtles
and snow-white Azaleas
that guard their shadows like mother hens.
The sun dries wigglers into contorted sculptures.

The cat uninterested in motionless toys
tiptoes across the damp lawn
shakes rainwater from its paws
climbs the front porch steps
and curls up next to a rocking chair
just outside the reach of shadows.

A Brief History of Square Pegs in Round Holes

by Mark Van Houten

There was a time when peg board games swept the nation. Remember? It's the game whereby the player inserts 3-inch-long pegs into holes arrayed on a wooden board. Some of the pegs are long rectangles with square ends, and the others are 3-inch-long cylinders with circular ends. The prototypes had all the squares lined up in rows at one end of the board, and the circulars at the other end.

For decades the pegboard game sat idle, collecting dust on distributor's shelves, because the board had a boringly uniform look. Popularity skyrocketed when controversy erupted from toy activists questioning the method of arraying the standard placement restrictions of pegs on the board, claiming it was too polarizing for children. Others claimed passionately that certain of the square pegs might self-identify as circular pegs and wanted them to be placed in the rows along with square pegs. Others wanted square and circular pegs to be distributed in a more socially equitable pattern over the board, preferably 6 inches apart, and that areas within the board should be proportional with a more equal mix of circular and square pegs.

The debate over the appropriate method of integrating the pegs became heated with opposing voices becoming increasingly aggressive. Police were called urgently to mediate disputes, when, for example, neighbors would mount flags featuring square pegs over their driveways in neighborhoods favoring round pegs. Peg riots broke out in many cities across America, so politicians redlined new peg friendly districts.

When the manufacturers recommended using a heavy hammer to violently force square pegs into round holes, rights activists at the ACLU took the manufacturers to court. Finally, the issue was decided by the Supreme Court in a close 5/4 decision, favoring the consumers. Representing the majority position the Chief Justice held the manufacturers in contempt of Diversity, Inclusion and Equity, and ordered the manufacturers to make the appropriate accommodations to integrate the pieces. Reparations were awarded to the plaintiffs in the form of refunds plus pain and suffering.

The manufacturers tried to accommodate varied consumers demands by designing pegs square on one side and round on the other. Yet some countered that this resulted in too many of one peg type, but not enough of the other hole type. Manufacturers then mixed square and circular features at branch points along the peg, so that each peg could insert into more than one type of adjacent hole. Unfortunately, consumers found the game had become too complex and confusing. Further, the assimilation attempt caused pieces to lose their original identities. The game dropped in popularity, and eventually most of the pegboards were burned in public bon fires across the nation.

Years later, nostalgic collectors across the nation would take their pegboard games out of storage for a yearly pegboard parade to commemorate the history of attempted pegboard integration. Many wore t-shirts showing square pegs or round pegs, but none with both, embarrassing the parade organizers. Gargantuan pegboards, the size of a football field, were constructed by the government for pegs of all types in public parks, at taxpayer expense. Coming full circle, manufacturers reaped huge profits from these ostentatious public displays. Sated activists moved on to cancel other pressing issues on social media.

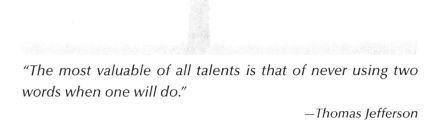

"The most valuable of all talents is that of never using two words when one will do."

—Thomas Jefferson

how to live
by Marissa C. Knox

today
I saw a bumblebee
nuzzled into
the iridescent petals
of an iris blooming
amidst the red poppy anemones,
orange wallflowers,
and pink tulips.

the bee rested in the embrace
of the purple and yellow flower
lost in ecstasy
lingering
drinking
savoring the nectar
for so long I thought it might have
died.
but it emerged wiggling,
covered in the sacred dust
of possibility.

dizzily
and delightfully
finding its way
to a new blossom
a new moment
in which to immerse
its whole being
and give its presence
and attention

fully
to the irresistible miracle
of what is
and then
receive
the mystery of what may be
to create
energy, abundance, beauty
to nurture
and nourish the glow of joy, and
love.
the sweetness of purpose
in divine presence.
an embodiment of magic
a meeting with source
transforming grace into life into grace.
and I wonder
how I might live
like a bumblebee.

A Weekend Silent Retreat

by Laura Miller

The table of silent women
makes a powerful sound.

A sisterhood of silence
cradled in the midst
of a still forest
at the edge of a noisy road.

We are the hushed forest,
containing each other
in our spiritual wombs
at the edge of a bellowing world.

Rescue Filly

by Sherrill A. Erickson

I had a call from my husband, Chief of the Building Department for the Hawaii County.

He told me he had to condemn a house. "There was a dead body in there. A woman."

"Oh, my god."

"The guy from the fire department told me this happens more than people realize. Someone moves over from the mainland. Gets a house and lands in paradise. Doesn't know anybody. Dies. Alone."

"Sad."

"It gets sadder."

"Oh?"

"She had a horse."

"Horse?"

"Palomino filly. Caught in barb wire."

"Oh, no."

He texted me a picture. She was lying on the grass like a blur of gold. I texted Send GPS. I'm coming.

As I rushed to leave, I glimpsed a few of my "rescues" swishing their tails in the afternoon light. The red roan appaloosa rodeo mare was a recovered founder case. Thumbelina survived a fractured cannon bone and her foreleg healed bent as a crooked stick. Then there was Licorice, a petting zoo reject that looked more like a dust mop than an equine.

I stowed leg wraps, medications, halter and rope, and a flake of hay in the hay bag. As I drove out, my "thinking" brain asserted itself, questioning the logic, or rather lack of logic, in another horse rescue. Time, money. Heartbreak.

For what? A second chance?

Last chance?

I made my way to a rough cinder road through mauka Hamakua pastures bordered by towering Eucalyptus. There were rusted metal gates to open and close. Rainwater filled potholes splashed up the side of my truck. My beater horse trailer bounced and I was glad the shocks at least were new. I could count on my husband to keep our vehicles in top shape. As if he knew I was thinking about him, my phone jingled as I hit a pothole so big it made my head hit the truck ceiling.

"Having fun?"

"Are you?"

"Vet called. Delayed."

"How is she?"

"Alive."

"Did you cut her free?"

"Working on it. ETA?"

"Ten minutes? Is she bleeding?"

"I've got pressure on the worst spot."

"How bad?"

"Not good."

I drove the rutted driveway through the open gate and saw the emergency vehicles. My husband's white Explorer. I slid alongside and jumped out.

As I hurried to the downed filly over whom my husband stood, I glanced at the house.

Overgrown. Neglected. The EMT crew had a body bag with someone in it on the stretcher they were loading into an ambulance. They were not in a hurry.

I felt a chill. *Death oh, death.* Shadowing the sun.

My husband, whose back was to me, turned, caught my eye, nodding slightly. I rushed toward him and knelt by the filly as he worked the dull wire cutters on the thick barb wire, bending the wire back and forth. Her sides heaving. Trapped.

I saw deep lacerations with hanging flaps of skin. Her neck. Her chest. Her flanks. Her ivory tail smeared with blood. How much blood could a horse lose?

Tears welled, but there was no time to indulge in emotion. My husband gestured for me to take over the pressure on the blood-soaked towel he held to her shoulder with his knee. Cutting away the tangled mass of barbed wire. Time.

There was not enough of it. If she fought as he worked to free her, she would lacerate herself further. And her flailing legs and sharp hooves could deliver a lethal kick. In her mind she was fighting for her life. She would give it everything. Everything she had left.

Sweat poured down my husband's red face as he battled the wire. Barbed wire had grazed his arm and a trickle of blood dried. The work was too fine for gloves. His fingers would be scratched all to hell. I touched his arm, looked into the filly's amber eyes. She had what horse people call *soft eyes*. Eyes indicative of a kind and willing temperament. Her pale eyelashes blinked once. Twice. She was holding on.

As the last strand of barbed wire was finally severed and sprung, she bled her life away unmoving. A pile of bones and hair. A Io (Hawaiian hawk) soared overhead. But for the cry of the Io, it was quiet. Dark clouds massing delivered a patter of rain.

I pushed down my hat, lowered my chin and felt tears trickle down my neck. Why had I come? Why oh, why. Just to see her bleed out?

My despair was interrupted by the throb of an engine. It was the vet, Dr. Smith. He wasted no time as he slammed his white Jeep into four-wheel drive and backed rapidly over the bumpy grass so that he was just a few feet from the filly. He hopped out with his burly assistant, Kamuela. I got out of the way as he rushed to check the filly's gums. They were white. Bad. Her capillary refill response was gone.

"She's going into shock."

"Get me the 10 gauge!"

He was speaking to Kamuela, but I felt myself get dizzy, as if I had lost all that blood.

"She needs fluids. Now!"

Kamuela leapt for the catheter and bag of saline solution. The Vet cannulated her jugular and inserted the catheter as Kamuela lifted the bag of fluids to the roof of the Vet's Jeep to increase flow and pressure.

"Not enough!"

He cannulated the other jugular, and Kamuela rigged up a second bag and catheter. It was a desperate, heroic measure to save the filly.

As the fluids entered her body, the Vet stanched bleeding lacerations with wads of gauze. Kamuela wielded the quart bottle of Betatine. He squirted, then took off the lid and dumped the entire red-brown solution into a tear on the filly's shoulder. I inhaled the pungent scent of iodine, the sound of surgical scissors clipping away jagged skin.

Death oh, death won't you spare her another day? The Vet tied off the ripped blood vessels in the deep chest wound, scissoring away the ragged layers of ripped tissue. He inserted a drainage tube, bringing clean edges of skin together, sewing them shut with needle and clear thread. He repeated this for lacerations on her hip, flank, and cheek. He checked her capillary refill time by pinching her skin.

Marginal.

He gave her a tetanus antitoxin, and 40 cc of penicillin, 20 cc in each hip. And a shot for the pain.

She was free of the barbed wire now, stitched up, and

medicated. Not moving. We watched her and waited. *Death oh death won't you spare . . .*

The sun had set when she finally struggled to rise, falling to her knees. Exhausted. She tried again. And again. Shaky. Very shaky. Bony girl with a matted coat. Not much to her at all. Kamuela leaned into her, steadying her.

"Atta girl."

"You can do it."

She let out a whinny that stabbed me in the heart, a hurt filly begging for her mother.

I got you.

I would bed her in clean straw. Attend to her wounds. But most important, with me, she would have friends. There would be other horses and ponies to answer her back.

When we got home.

"Fill your paper with the breathings of your heart."

—*William Wordsworth*

Ladybug

(A short children's poetic story)
by Nicole Sandoval Gurgone

Red and black
Black and red
Round as a circle
do you know who I am…
I am a ladybug
red and black.
The dots on my back tell you how
old I am.
The little bug looks so sad
counting frantically
each dot he gets sadder.
Why so sad, my little
bug?
You're getting older,
I feel I have less and less
time with you.
I feel so sad,
So sad and blue.
Mama ladybug looks down
And arches her wings around the little bug
I am here now and that is what matters.
Each day we treasure
Each year we will remember
Memories will last us forever
Always and forever
I will be in your heart.
Now look down at your wings they are shaped
in my heart.

To the Perfect Girls

by Jade Marie Smith

To all the girls
I'm proud of your confidence
Your smile that has no limit of shine
Your ribcage that doesn't bugle out each time you breathe in
   the air you need to survive
Your eyelashes that have no clumps
Your stomach that's perfect in every size
I wish I could steal your body and use it as my own
I wish there was no pressure to look and do as we are told
I hope to one day have your confidence
To look in the mirror and see no flaws
I truly hope you are happy with your looks
No one deserves to not love every inch of their body
They are supposed to own.
P.S. I love you.

"One day I will find the right words, and they will be simple."
—Jack Kerouac, *The Dharma Bums*

A Summer in New Orleans

by Margaret de Jaham

Between my Sophomore and Junior years in college, my father got me a job as a bookkeeper in a restaurant in the New Orleans French Quarter. A bookkeeper? Imagine that! My math skills were non-existent, but the thought of such a new adventure was a siren call I answered.

While in New Orleans, I lived in a home owned by an elderly lady from Pau, France. She had married a rich Italian, who made a fortune in New Orleans real estate. She spoke no English and had never left the Quarter in her 60 years of marriage. She would question me about how people protected themselves from the cowboys and Indians once they left the French Quarter and ventured out into the wide, scary world beyond. I loved her and her endearing old world ways.

My second story balcony overlooked the famous Lafitte's Blacksmith Shop, where the pirate Jean Lafitte met with friends while in town. He is said to be the person who inspired the main character in the movie Pirates of the Caribbean. This little bar is a favorite subject of artists and photographers from around the world.

Walking the five blocks to work in my high heels, dodging the water sprayed by the cleaning trucks, I savored the sights and sounds of mornings in the Quarter. The vendors brought produce in a spectrum of colors, and men arrived with fresh fish and seafood from the Gulf. They supplied the renowned restaurants of New Orleans, to which people flock to enjoy some of the best food in the world. The smell of fresh coffee and beignets being prepared in the Cafe du Monde permeated the air.

The tourists, still sleeping in their fancy hotels, would

gather later to relive their night of revelry on Bourbon Street. A night or two in the Big Easy! No one forgets that experience. Most would have failed to notice the highly sophisticated, elegantly dressed natives, who carry themselves with dignity and exhibit very courtly behavior. These are the people who have standing reservations at the best restaurants and, after dining, retire to their lush courtyards, hidden behind the high brick walls of the Quarter. They finish the night with a glass of Courvoisier, Grand Marnier, or perhaps a Brandy Alexander.

Arriving at the restaurant on the corner of Bourbon and Bienville Streets, I enter the dining room where preparations are in progress for luncheon guests. White linen tablecloths, the finest silver and crystal, bouquets of fresh flowers are at every table. The waiters are in tuxedos and the Creole women, dressed in elegant clothes, are of exquisite beauty.

Ascending the staircase to my office, I admire the original oil paintings that line the wall and the sight of the bustling staff below. Opening the door, I survey the chaotic scene and again wonder how they could have not done the books for March, April and May and still stay in business. Later I would learn that there was a second set of books I never saw.

Using an adding machine, I punch the keys, trying to bring order to the chaos of profit and loss. My head is spinning, and I wish once again that they had hired me to do something easy like write a ten-page essay on the philosophy of Voltaire.

Lunchtime at last. I pick up the phone and call down to the kitchen to order a cup of Turtle Soup and an entree of Trout Amandine. I realize that I have a cushy job.

The lunch crowd has thinned, and the bustle slows down in the hot, humid, summer afternoon. Everything will speed up soon as preparations for dinner begin.

After work, I walk home, admiring the paintings of the street artists and listening to the soft sounds of afternoon jazz. The Mississippi River gleams in the afternoon sun.

My landlady and I sit on the front stoop as evening falls. We watch the garbage trucks come to empty the trash cans, which are hidden under manhole covers in the streets. We discuss the problems of cowboys and Indians once again.

By the end of the summer, I have fallen fully under the spell of the New Orleans French Quarter, so full of history and charm. This is a place that embraces and encourages its colorful, talented residents, who prefer to dwell under the radar of tourism.

For me, this was a time of innocence and beauty, and that special summer is one of the many reasons New Orleans continues to occupy a place in my heart.

Every Mother is Afraid

by Nancy Pfaffl

We didn't realize

there would be a war.

Never considered

our beautiful city

Mariupol

Would be destroyed.

Artillery fire

Bombs exploding.

Smoke and ash.

A city under siege.

Snow falls gently.

Snowflakes cover

burned up shells

of tanks.

Like frosted toys

On a cake of white.

Piles of rubble

where buildings

collapsed.

Died.

Schools gone

Stores flattened

Homes destroyed

Churches became

    shelters

Parks became

      graveyards.

We are hungry.

We are cold.

Separated from our men

But holding on.

Where to get food?

How to obtain water?

What to do with the

   human waste?

When will sirens

   start up again?

Should we hide?

How to calm

   the children?

What will happen

  tomorrow?

How to get through

  today?

Receiving support

Leaning on each other.

Still a community.

One step

  In front of

    The next.

For Mariupol

For Ukraine

For our children.

For a future.

(Inspired by Taisiia, a mother in Ukraine)

the night my father died

by Paula Shaffer Robertson

the night my father died
i dreamt i disappeared

like a withered flower
pale on this withering day

petal crumb on a doily napkin
to briskly whisk away

no more reason
to fill up this empty space

emotions merged
into a darker plane

my non-existence
defined acutely clear

this complex man
of mangled dreams

destroyer of his
american dream

so unamerican

family betrayer
family slayer

guilt-ridden name

these pangs of grief
released no salty tears

for a man i loved
from a distant sphere

questions unanswered
locked inside

who is this man
who at the end

consumes my life?

this loveless man
branded with rage

unable to give

unforgiving
unforgivable

inexcusable

so in the end …

i could not cry
the night my father died

"None of us, including me, ever do great things. But we can all do small things, with great love, and together we can do something wonderful."

—*Mother Teresa*

The Ball Sticks to My Feet

by Ghaffar Pourazar

As a college senior in the UK, I became demoralized and sickened by the Iran-Iraq war at home. I escaped into socializing and drinking, letting my university studies and my beloved soccer game suffer.

One night after leaving the pub with my soccer club friends, we headed to Raj's Curry House in Manchester, where I joined in a challenge to see who could eat the spiciest curry on the menu, called 'Suicide Curry.' I accepted the challenge. But then, I felt an ocean wave hit me just as I finished the fiery mixture. Running outside, I became violently ill. As I lay in my sweat on a side street, my friend and soccer team captain Dave sat with me. Dave, a chubby ginger-haired Liverpudlian, had convinced me to join the soccer club; I guess he felt responsible for me.

"All this drinking? What's going on?" Dave asked.

"It's the war—my mum couldn't transfer funds. I can't pay my bills and college fees."

Dave didn't laugh or put me off.

He said, "It must be painful to be rich and not have access to your money."

"It wasn't always like that. My parents were tailors. We struggled in my early childhood, but it was still full of joy. By the time I was ten, the family's lingerie business was busy and successful. I even had to open the store on weekends and sell bras."

"How fun. What was that like?"

"Can you imagine? I was shy, and the ladies often didn't know their size, so I had to guess for them. I'd spot them coming, quickly size 'em up and pull out the box with their size before they could get to the counter. It was crazy. The economy was booming, and Mum & Dad were successful enough to send me and my younger siblings here or the US for our educations within a few years."

I told Dave more than I'd told anyone about how my parent's good fortune didn't last. "With the regime change, the store was often targeted by the local police. My mum told me about a local cop who regularly visited the store, berated my parents, levied heavy fines, and loaded up with as much lingerie as he could pack in a suitcase. My parents were powerless to stop him. They had no choice but to sell the shop for the highest dollar and emigrate."

"What? That sucks, but you got away early."

"I was thirteen when I left Tehran in 1974. I joined my aunt in Cambridge and went to a private school. When in Cambridge, I was adopted by the Chinese society on campus by chance or fate. They loved me for my soccer skills and sense of humor. My Malaysian, Indonesian, and Hong Kong roommates taught me the pleasures of Chinese tea, cooking, and mahjong. They taught me super skills in badminton and took me to Jackie Chan movies. They kept remarking: "You were Chinese in your past life.""

"Wow. I'd never left Liverpool before university. All I can say is that you've had an interesting life."

I felt encouraged to tell him the rest of what was on my mind.

"My cousin, Amir, was conscripted and sent to the front. Now he's missing."

"Man, sorry to hear that. No wonder you're feelin so crappy; Were you close?"

"Yeah, he's the eldest of my cousins, always joking around. He taught me many fun things. Amir is lanky and plays soccer in flip-flops." I laughed.

"You're joking."

"I called him toop be pash michasbeh."

"What does that mean?"

"It means: the ball sticks to his feet. The first time I saw him dribble the ball past four opponents, I froze."

"Why?"

"Simple, he was fast, passing to the wall and receiving it once he was past the opponent. He just repeated the one-two with the wall, and any teammate he passed to, became a wall."

"What was that phrase again?"

"Toop be pash michasbeh."

Dave repeated it over and over as he walked away. It felt good to tell someone about Amir.

Before the next game, Dave held my arm tight. "Max is injured. You take the midfield. You can do this!" His voice was firm, but his gaze was warm and brotherly.

As I started dribbling the ball past opponents, Dave shouted, "Toop be pash michasbeh."

An Englishman pronounces these Sanskrit-like words in a hilarious Scouse accent. He must have planned this carefully. The phrase transported me back to childhood when my cousins and I played in the "kucheh" alleyways dodging bicycles and motorbikes veering left, right, and center during our games. Amir and I dominated with our ability to do the one-two with the ball. We exchanged signals and quick words as we passed the ball.

"Bedeh," give, Amir shouted and sped past the opponent.

"Boro," go, I shouted and released the ball.

"Male-man," mine, I said as I separated from the opponent demanding the ball.

"Male-to," yours, Amir releases.

Suddenly, in my mind, my teammates on the field became my cousin Amir. I couldn't make a wrong move. The opponents didn't know what hit them with our quick one-two passes. I set up my colleagues and even scored goals myself. Thanks to Dave, my performance on the field continued for the rest of the year.

After this success, I started focusing on my studies with only a few weeks to catch up. I needed to raise my test scores, particularly in math, to receive a Bachelor's Degree in Electronic Computer Systems. Whew! My academic life fell into place, and my soccer game returned.

The best news came when I heard from my mum about Amir. My Uncle Ayoub had pulled every string he could and found Amir in a hospital near the war zone. Upon Amir's release, he decided to escape Iran via Turkey. Eventually, he obtained refugee status in Germany.

Amir's words still ring in my head: "Once you start a war, the results are only destruction, and no one can control the events which follow."

At the final club gala that year, I dressed nicely in a dark tie and a light-green colored suit. The annual event was held in a large hall in the student's union building. This was my last gala as I was graduating. After dinner and speeches, Dave stood up, threw me a witty smile, and started announcing the annual club awards.

"The man of the year award goes to Ghaffar Pourazar."

Shocked, I couldn't move or even lift my head.

Now, at age sixty, having received several international awards, including the Key to Bejing from the Mayor, receiving the Man of the Year Award, the most unexpected award of my life. I'd experienced the college student's life with more joys and hardships than most but always struggled to find real friends. And Dave's sincere friendship proved I was absolutely wrong; I finally felt included. Even now, I am humbled by this award, which proved to me that I belonged.

The sound of applause brought me out of myself as I approached Dave, with my head up, to collect my award.

rest here
by Marissa C. Knox

snow rests
where it can be held.
it lands
softly
slowly
silently
in the embrace
of a
naked branch.

fallen trees
offer their
mossy shade.

the open ground
invites each crystal
to arrive
in its spacious field
of loving awareness.

quietly and
together
it grows deeper
and enriches the brightness
of its velvety blanket
that keeps us warm
in a hearth of enchantment.

awe like a flame
illuminating the inner sparkle
of each fallen flake
swirling and resting-
soft and radiant.

i listen to the stilling motion
the flurries of stardust
misting and mixing
with my breath.

i hear nothing.
i feel everything.

a twinkle of cold
upon my cheek
like a kiss from a tiny angel.

i am here too,
merging with the
glitter as it descends.
floating in wonder,
i rise up to meet the source,
lifting my heart
toward the sky.

i allow myself to rest
in the midst of this luminous cloud
that i find myself within
where i remember the entire cosmos.
yes this is where i shall rest
like a rainbow rests in light,
like a snowflake rests in flight.

Finding Forgiveness

by Kimberly Krantz

There are no medals awarded here.
Is it God that says to forgive and forget? Or was that Mom?
As a child, I only remember looking up at the voice.

Thinking about many times, cruel words, and a broken heart.
I am angry and hurt.

Some due to the name-calling, body-shaming, and bullying.
Some from family or so-called friends who abandoned me to
    fight on my own.

I think I forgot a lot - which is good;
but old wounds still bleed - which is bad.

Because
I have not yet found forgiveness,
I keep searching,
I need more time.

This poem is based on the prompt:
"For which act of forgiveness do you deserve a medal?"

"Write about small, self-contained incidents that are still vivid in your memory. If you remember them, it's because they contain a larger truth that your readers will recognize in their own lives. Think small and you'll wind up finding the big themes in your family saga."

—William Zinsser

Tender Nights Revisited

by JG McCrillis

I long to lie alongside you

your presence whispering
gentle warmth

breath suspiring soft
in easy slumber

hint of chamomile
in your hair

candlelight's gilded glow
upon your shoulder

serene sensation, touching you
like touching satin

luxurious length, body
beside body

Erato's lyre, quiet musing
our lips last rendezvous
lingering

I descend into the hollow breach
the empty space

the place

where you

are not

tonight

Keeper of Your Secrets

by Jade Marie Smith

I'm the keeper of your secrets
The one that keeps you sane
I hold all your broken promises
All of your pain
I'm the keeper of your safety
The one you tell all your truth to
All your unspoken words
The ones that will always be there
I hold all your battles inside me
While keeping all mine hidden
I hold all my things in
Just to let you be okay
I keep all my secrets within for your own protection
I'm the keeper of your secrets
Of your wicked ways
You put me through this heartache
You put me through your own personal pain
I feel like the walls are caving in
My own safe is breaking within
I'm your one and only outlet
Cursed with all your hidden sides
I'm the keeper of your lies
Your broken-hearted ways
I hold on to this key while you put it all in my safe
And I hope you're happy now
Knowing I will never be the same
After knowing all that you hide inside
After keeping you
Safe.
P.S. I love you.

"A blank piece of paper is God's way of telling us how hard it is to be God."

—*Sidney Sheldon*

Mrs. Roosevelt Comes to Dinner

by MaryAnn Easley

When I was young, my mother never missed President Franklin D. Roosevelt's Fireside Chats. After December 7th, she and the neighbors turned on radios in the evening so that his voice resonated between our houses. Anyone strolling Woodbine Street could follow the thread of his message; it must have been that way throughout Los Angeles.

President Roosevelt reassured my mother and the rest of America that he'd take care of us if we did our part. My father left his teaching job to join the Navy; my brother Jack and I collected tinfoil; our mother planted a Victory Garden; Grandma saved bacon grease; everyone doled out ration stamps for precious gas, sugar, flour, meat.

Roosevelt won our allegiance.

My mother cried when he died.

In 1960, my father, now President of a community college, entered the house with exciting news. "Sarah, how would you like to have Mrs. Roosevelt come for dinner?"

My mother's eyes shone. "Eleanor?"

My father explained that the former First Lady had been invited to speak at the college.

Mrs. Roosevelt had become a force; she'd served as a delegate to the United Nations and chaired the Human Rights Commission and the Commission on the Status of Women.

My father said he'd already invited key faculty members and student leaders for dinner."Nineteen in all."

"At our table?"

"Faculty can't leave wives at home," my father said. "The student body president and newspaper editor have girlfriends. We'll bring in extra chairs."

Since she lived downstairs, Grandma overheard and

joined in. "Wendell? What's this? Eleanor Roosevelt is coming for dinner?"

My mother's mind must have been racing. Jack and I were grown with agendas of our own, but what about our nine-year-old brother Billy? And our sister, Wendy Jean, who had never been quite right? If Grandma had an invitation, then Aunt Tillie, Mama's sister who lived in Long Beach, couldn't be ignored.

My mother had crosses to bear. One was Grandma, her judgmental mother-in-law; another was Wendy—born with Down Syndrome—who could not interact in polite company. And Aunt Tillie, of course, wouldn't miss a chance to meet Eleanor Roosevelt.

My father believed in my mother's ability to handle anything. He said he could see God in my mother's eyes, and that's how it was with them.

He planned to drive to the Beverly Hills residence where Mrs. Roosevelt would be staying, pick her up late afternoon, and bring her back to the house prior to her lecture.

My mother gasped. "In our old station wagon?"

He let out a breath. "I thought you'd be pleased. You mean, you don't want her to come?"

She reached out. "Oh, no . . . anyone else would scare me to death but not Eleanor."

For Eleanor, my mother would scour the floors, wash the good China, extend the table, bring in extra chairs, figure out a menu, deal with Wendy, and buy groceries. She wrung her hands, smoothed her apron, and got out her Betty Crocker cookbook, fingering one page after another.

Pearl Buck, Margaret Mead, Alex Haley, Ray Bradbury, Louis Leakey, and Allen Ginsberg had all lectured at the college, but my father had never invited any of those notables for dinner. "It's fun to meet such people," he said.

"And learn they're not much different than us common folk."

Even though bedazzled, my mother decided on dessert—lemon meringue pie fit for a queen—and then she started her shopping list: lemons, flour, sugar, eggs, shortening . . .

As planned, my father drove the station wagon to collect Mrs. Roosevelt and her female secretary in Beverly Hills. The former First Lady immediately quipped, "Everywhere I go, people look at me and seem to think they know me."

Her secretary laughed as my father joined in. The ice broken, he headed southwest to point out the vibrant streaks of sunset along the coast.

"Did you tell me what my subject is for tonight?" Mrs. Roosevelt asked her secretary.

Laughter again, and my father had to confess that he labored over every speech.

Mrs. Roosevelt told him that the first time she stood up to speak, she shook with fear. Her advisor suggested never writing her words down but simply organizing the main points. "He told me, 'When you've said what you have to say—sit down.'"

They laughed like friends.

He didn't mention that we never discussed religion or politics when guests came to dinner. This rule was established after arguments with my uncle, a lawyer from Whittier. In addition, Grandma's strait-laced views about sin and salvation terrified the younger generations; her critiques extended to my mother and the rest of us. Being an election year with a Catholic running for office, I wondered how either topic could be avoided.

Once exiting the family's old Chevy, Mrs. Roosevelt strode into the house, noticed guests lined up in her honor, and went from one to another, shaking hands. "Hello, I'm Eleanor Roosevelt."

To get her two cents in, Grandma mentioned she'd once been a suffragette.

The student body president interrupted with a prepared thought. "I'm curious," he said, "how does someone like Mrs. Roosevelt choose a presidential candidate?"

"Stay curious," Eleanor said. "We never stop learning." She preferred a mature candidate, someone who didn't think in absolutes, someone with humility. "In this world, we need more love and charity."

Even though it broke our dinner talk rule, this set the tone as everyone gathered around the table. Aunt Tillie, dressed in a frilly white apron, brought over the serving bowl filled with Mama's scalloped potatoes.

"A politician should be a statesman," Mrs. Roosevelt continued. "Interested in big questions; he should never miss an opportunity to meet new people and learn new things."

The college newspaper editor, less prepared than his colleague, seemed to want to take notes; he checked a pocket and then took a gulp from his water glass.

My father came to his rescue. "At the college, we're fortunate to have individuals from many different environments, races, and cultures."

The editor found his voice, repeating what he'd heard my father say. "The future depends upon us getting along and helping one another."

My father never treated anyone lesser than himself; he may have been college president, but he wasn't above bending over to pick up trash or dog poop to keep the campus tidy. He would have placed Wendy at the table if my mother would have agreed.

After plates were cleared, my mother brought out dessert. Peaks of meringue crowned four pies; crust edges, uniformly pinched by thumb, resembled art.

"Lemon pie," a faculty wife exclaimed.

"Homemade," my mother confessed.

No one refused a slice.

When dinner concluded, my father asked Mrs. Roosevelt if he could assist her when she ascended the stage later.

"Oh, mercy, no." She sprang to her feet to prove her point, acknowledged everyone by name, thanked my mother, and then looked for Billy.

"He'll be along," my father said. "We'll all be attending the lecture."

"Even Billy? I didn't want to miss saying goodbye."

Perhaps she wouldn't have really minded meeting Wendy who was ensconced downstairs with her own piece of pie.

I think Mrs. Roosevelt would have spoken to her in a nice way.

"Almost anyone can be an author; the business is to collect money and fame from this state of being."

—A. A. Milne

Fissure

by William Black

I should have recognized, three years in,
after studying the scale of separation,
inviting acceptance, searching forgiveness,
and facing, finally, my own seismic faults,
that you were not returning.
I would spend what my sister called the last chapter
alone.

I should have known that the old man you visited
during your stint in hospice work,
the one we used to muse about,
sitting alone at the small table in his pale kitchen
where the fractured cabinet doors no longer fit,
would be me.

Each interface of us,
every touch, smile or embrace brought me lingering hope,
a small wave across a dry riverbed,
but, in the end, only
a litter of poems
across a fragile ground.

I should have learned, somehow,
three years before now,
the redefinition you sought was enduring,
the surprise, most of all, that the epicenter was me.

La Rosa

by Laura Miller

Oh! you fancy fibonacci.
Ruffled profusion,
edges aflutter
in the slightest breeze.

A rosy blush
I wish for my cheek.
A gentle invitation
to steal a kiss.

Nestled in the fairy circle,
dusted with powdered sun,
held aloft by sturdy stems
as thorny as new love.

"In the company of flowers, we know happiness. In the company of trees, we are able to think."

—*John Stewart Collis*

A Simple Act of Kindness

by Angela Tippell

George made his bed, folding his pajamas and putting them neatly under the pillow, then made his way to the kitchen. He sat by the window with his mug of tea and piece of toast, to determine the weather. Trees swaying slightly, bit of a breeze, but bright, not too bad for sitting outside. Later, he'd put on a scarf and enjoy being outdoors at a table of *The George & Dragon Pub*, overlooking the river Thames.

The pub had been a regular watering hole for many years when Maisie was alive.

"I'm George and you're the Dragon," he'd joke with her.

Maisie, far from being a dragon, but a more sweet and gentle soul you'd ever wish to meet. She'd have made a lovely mum, everyone said. They had both wished for children, but it was never meant to be.

George and Maisie enjoyed their own company and that of friends and family, but now Maisie was gone. As were their siblings and most of their friends. George especially now, wished he had children and grandchildren to share memories with.

The past fifteen months he'd settled into the routine of a single person. Tidy the flat in the mornings, make a sandwich, then catch the bus from the corner of the street to go to *The George & Dragon Pub,* Mondays through Fridays, where he'd have a half pint of beer to go with the sandwich he'd made.

On his way home, stopping at the supermarket to pick up one or two items. He spread his shopping out, so he could go in every day. This way he could chat to the young man who stocked the shelves and the nice ladies who sat at the check-out. A little bit of company before he returned to his flat and the lonely hours ahead.

Every other Saturday the women's volunteer group at the church put on a coffee morning for seniors. George enjoyed going there for an hour having a coffee and a biscuit. The other two Saturdays of the month, his niece, Sally, would come over to visit. She'd do some odds and ends for him, things he missed Maisie doing, sew on buttons or darn a sweater. Sally would always bring a nice treat, packet of chocolate biscuits or a cake. They'd sit and chit chat about family matters.

'Funny that,' he thought. 'Family matters. Not much family these days. Odd really, him and Maisie both having come from large families. All scattered or gone now. Two nephews in America and another niece married, living in Australia. Only got Sally now, she didn't live that close, and had her own kids to tend to. Still, she was a good girl. Always did right by him at Christmas and his birthday, invited him go to stay with her for a few days.'

George started to make his sandwich. He opened a tin of Spam and placed it on the cutting board. He measured two perfectly matched slices, leaving enough to cut two more slices over the following two days. Two tins of spam a week made him six sandwiches. On Sundays he treated himself to something special. He would walk to the corner shop and buy a paper, a weekly treat. Then come home and prepare a Kipper with brown bread and butter for his Sunday breakfast.

Wrapping up his sandwich, George placed it carefully in his jacket pocket, checked he had his senior citizen bus pass, put on his flat cap and scarf and set off for the bus stop.

The *George & Dragon Pub* overlooked the river Thames, it had a lovely outdoor seating area. There were long wooden tables with benches, and a few individual tables and chairs. Large pots with conifers placed around, baskets hung from the eaves along the back of the pub. In the Spring and Summer, they were filled with red Geraniums, white Petunias and blue Lobelia. A patriotic splash of color, most appropriate as St. George, the patron saint of England had slayed the Dragon, the peril of England.

George made his way along the Embankment to the pub. Going to the bar, he greeted the publican.

"Morning Tom. How's it going for you?"

"Can't complain, and yourself George? The usual?"

George took his half pint of beer and found his usual spot in the corner of the patio at a table for two. He settled himself down for a pleasant hour, he never stayed longer. One he couldn't afford another drink and he knew when the lunch time crowd came the tables would be needed for folks to sit, to eat the pub lunches they'd purchased. If the weather was cold, he'd find a table in the corner of the pub and eat his homemade sandwich. George was always very discreet with eating it, he didn't think Tom noticed, being so busy at the bar, but he wouldn't push his luck.

The lunch crowd started to drift in, some seated inside and others bringing their drinks and food to the patio. Young people, office workers, middle management types, women as well as men. Very different to his younger days when a woman wouldn't have gone to a pub without a man. So nice to see a mix of young people enjoying their lunch break. Three men came and sat at a long table with their drinks. Two young women, at a table for two, their heads together chatting.

George sat looking at the river, at low tide that day, he watched several gulls pecking around in the mud. Suddenly an overhead gull swooped down beside him.

"Blimey." He cried out as the gull made off with the best part of his lunch in his beak.

The women turned and giggled. The three men glanced over, one said, "Bad luck mate." Another of the men registered the crestfallen look on George's face as he got up to go into the pub to pick up their lunch order. At the bar, he remarked to Tom.

"Poor old bloke out there had his sandwich nicked by a bloody gull."

"Ah, that would be George," Tom said, as he pulled three pints. "He comes in here every week day, brings his own sandwich." He put the three lunches on a tray. "I never say anything, he obviously can't afford more than his half pint. He stays less than an hour. Used to come in with his wife regularly. She passed away a year or so ago. I think he's lonely and comes in here to remember her."

As the young man got out his money to pay for the lunches, he said,

"Put a hot sausage roll and whatever it is he drinks on our bill."

The man carried the lunches out, then brought the sausage roll and beer over to George. "Saw what that thieving gull did. Hope you don't mind, took the liberty of getting you this and some beer to wash it down."

George looked up and thanked him.

"No need to have done that mate ... but cheers. Thank you."

George gazed out over the river; tears clouded his eyes from the simple act of kindness.

"If you don't have time to read, you don't have the time (or the tools) to write. Simple as that."

—*Stephen King*

Ready, Set, Go

by Sheila Roell

When my dad died unexpectedly on a business trip, I was 18 years old, a college freshman. I was devastated and in a state of disbelief. When I returned to school, I had trouble functioning and lived in a fog. I dropped out of college, isolated myself, and spent most of my time sleeping. I worked at Dow Chemical, but I was complacent, going through the motions, joyless, without any zest for living. I seemed to be waiting for something.

Then, my friends took up the sport of parachute jumping. And I felt excited for the first time in a while. Why not try skydiving, I thought.

A month later, I'm kneeling on the floor of an old Piper Cub airplane. What am I doing? Am I going to parachute out of this airplane? The inside of the plane seems barren, stripped of its seats and soundproofing. Even the door is missing. The engine's deafening buzzing noise prevents conversation.

The weight of my parachute sets me back on my heels as the plane climbs to our jump altitude of approximately 4,000 feet. I'm alert but wrapped in fear. Am I going to do this? I glance at the other six jumpers with me. We're all wearing parachutes packed by a person we don't know. Yikes. The long training day is behind us, and graduation is our first jump. We are focused and serious. Are they as afraid as me? Jumping out of an airplane is wild and crazy and perhaps stupid. But I no longer feel complacent. I bargain with God and promise to finish school if I live through this. My surge of panic is interrupted by Mike, motioning me forward.

Am I first? Oh no. Yet my body moves into the gaping

hole where the door used to be. Mike yells.

"READY."

I scoot further into the vast opening in the side of the plane, sticking my legs out. The wind immediately whisks them to the side.

I focus on the back of Mike's head and arm. Mike's concentrating on the pilot. His arm waves motioning the pilot to cut the engine. It's suddenly dead quiet. My legs no longer have to fight the wind and dangle free.

It's my moment of truth.

"SET."

Mike yells, and I lean into the opening with only one butt cheek gripping the edge of the plane. I might fall.

"GO."

It's the last thing I hear. I tip out of the plane and arch my back as taught. Immediately, my static line opens my chute, and I feel the sudden jerk upward as the canopy fills with air. I'm in control. I can't see the airplane or hear a sound. I'm afloat.

I maneuver my toggles, as we learned in class. They work perfectly. I can turn left or right or make a circle. I'm alive at this moment. In less than 90 seconds, I'm over the jump target, and it's time to descend. Using the toggles, I close all the vents as I turn until I feel the wind on my face and prepare to land.

Looking down, I see my brother and sister-in-law trying to capture me on their cameras. I call out, "Steve!" as I float overhead.

Lifting my knees into a crouch position, I remember Mike's warning, "Don't tense; relax your body." I see the ground approaching fast. Bang!

I hit the ground hard, rolling across my lower leg, hip, back, and shoulder. I absorb the landing pretty well. It feels great to jump up and signal I'm okay. I gather my chute before it can drag me down the freshly plowed farmer's field.

Farmer's field? Oh no, I missed the drop zone by a bit.

Who cares? I feel exhilaratingly alive.

A yellow jeep driven by a ground crew member arrives to pick me up. I unclamp my chute, toss it in the back, and climb into the front seat.

"Great Jump." The driver, an experienced jumper himself, hands me a small plastic baggie containing orange slices.

"Thanks." I didn't realize I was thirsty.

We drive back to the jump station, where I watch the rest of my classmates make their first jump. Mike makes the final jump as we all watch our master. He lands with flair.

Mike signs everyone's jump card and presents each of us with a jump log book. We laugh and joke for a few minutes congratulating each other on our daring feat.

And then, it's over.

Later that night, I relive the experience and think of my dad. I am clear about my life for the first time since his death. Dad, wherever he is, is also with me. I admire the cover of my leather-bound jump book and envision my second jump—no more shuffling through life. I'll finish school and embrace living. I will be the daughter Dad always knew I could be.

"A book is made from a tree. It is an assemblage of flat, flexible parts (still called "leaves") imprinted with dark pigmented squiggles. One glance at it and you hear the voice of another person, perhaps someone dead for thousands of years. Across the millennia, the author is speaking, clearly and silently, inside your head, directly to you. Writing is perhaps the greatest of human inventions, binding together people who never knew each other, citizens of distant epochs. Books break the shackles of time. A book is proof that humans are capable of working magic."

—Carl Sagan

THE WRITERS COLLECTIVE
MEET THE AUTHORS

Jennifer Black, M.D., has been a board-certified hospice and palliative medicine physician for 25 years. She received national and regional community service awards from Kaiser Permanente for her work providing education to healthcare professionals and laypersons about hospice, palliative medicine, and advance care planning. She has written several published editorials and participated in community forums and educational events about these topics, as well as medical aid in dying (MAID) and abortion care. She resides in Portland, OR.

Jim Black is a lawyer, writer, and cartoonist from Southern California. Jim's background includes working as a photographer for several daily newspapers, as an on-air radio personality on stations in California, and writing for newspapers and special interest magazines. His short stories, articles, and cartoons can be seen in various publications.

William Black an emeritus university administrator and writer. He co-founded Dads2Dads, an initiative devoted to recognizing the challenges of fatherhood and improving the skills of dads. He is a devoted father and grandfather and the author of *Dads2Dads: Tools for Raising Teenagers* and *Grit and Grace: Black Fathers Tell Their Stories*. He works at living a thoughtful, mindful, and helpful life.

 **Momoyo Capanna** is an active member of several writing groups: Creative Journaling, Word Weavers, and Haiku San Diego. She is also a member of the Haiku Society of America. Her poems and haiku have been published in the *California Quarterly, Modern Haiku, Dragonfly*, and several haiku, Hai bun, and creative writing anthologies. She enjoys composing shahai, a combination of her haiku with her photographs. A retired high school guidance counselor, she lives in San Clemente with her terrier mix dog, Lacey.

 **Melinda Cohen** has been fascinated with writing since reading her first novel at age 12. This blossomed into journal writing, short stories, and nonfiction articles. Her love of animals led to a published monthly column in her community magazine featuring pets and their owners. As a grateful member of MaryAnn Easley's critique groups, Melinda is close to completing her first novel. She enjoys editing her fellow writer friends' projects and assists at a women's workout studio with their weekly online newsletter. She also interviews clients of that business to share their fitness journeys with others.

Julie Crandall writes for healing and self-discovery. Several of her stories dealing with her experience with breast cancer were published in Barbara Delinsky's *UPLIFT, Secrets from the Sisterhood of Breast Cancer Survivors*. She is a WFAE writing award recipient and has compiled a dozen collections of short stories and meditations. Julie is actively involved in two tightly knit writing critique groups, finding inspiration from writers all over the country through Zoom. She is a preschool teacher and loves tutoring and sharing her love of reading and writing with children of all ages.

Margaret de Jaham taught French language and literature at the university and high school levels. Her academic writings are in libraries in the United States and France. Now retired, she is actively involved in creative journaling and writing critique groups, where she enjoys writing short memoir pieces.

MaryAnn Easley award-winning author and educator is the recipient of the Junior Library Guild Selection Award and the Greater San Diego Reading Association Award for her novel *I Am the Ice Worm*. MaryAnn was chosen twice as Teacher of the Year and received the Career Achievement Award from the University of Redlands. Author of more than a dozen novels and several nonfiction books, she won two first-place prizes in Story Circle Network's 2022 Poetry and Life-Writing Competitions. She resides and teaches in Laguna Niguel, where she's actively involved in helping writers reach their full creative potential.

Sherrill A. Erickson has a passion for books and enjoys writing creatively in her spare time. Publication credits include *Equus Magazine*, *Hawaii Pacific Review*, and *Interstices An Anthology*. An attorney and licensed broker, she's currently working on a novel, *Mana Road* as a participant in a fiction/poetry critique group. She has a degree in Sociology from the University of Washington, a Horsemastership from Kokohead Stables in Hawaii, and a law degree from UCLA, where she was Associate Editor of Law Review. She lives in Hawaii with her husband Neil and her six horses: Double D, Braveheart, Dancer, Melani, Midnight, and Kamuela.

Nicole Sandoval Gurgone is a teaching assistant and a frequent guest speaker in middle schools in Chicago, inspiring young people to write. She writes poetry and short stories for children and has been featured in the local library. Actively involved in a critique group, she also attends writing retreats, networks with other writers, and believes in the transformative power of journal and poetry writing for people of all ages. Nicole resides in the Chicagoland area with her husband and three sons.

J. Hanson writes fiction, creative nonfiction, and screenplays. She has published her poetry and a debut novel, *Pinwheels*, and has won awards for her fiction. An editor, script consultant, co-creator and co-host of Bite the Pen, a podcast about storytelling in all mediums, she is a strong advocate of fanfiction and has wide-ranging experience in the art of writing and storytelling.

John Henning begins his writing process by taking notes. Combining and interchanging summaries of general interest research, experiences, and observations produce some original fictional concepts, but structure and style is also needed to create engaging stories. For the past several years, he's participated in a writer's critique circle, where he receives positive creative support and technical critiques from the circle members. This, along with his determined efforts, have helped him develop the craft of storytelling. He's currently finishing a rough draft of a novel he expects to complete this year.

Peggy Jaffe actively participates in a writer's critique group in Laguna Niguel, California. One of her memoir essays, *Pricier than Prada,* was published in the anthology *Leave the Lipstick, Take the Iguana*, which won a bronze award. For inspiration, she frequently draws on her enchantment and the challenges of living in the Tuscan countryside for more than twenty years.

Anna Jevne (aka Joanna Jacobs) is a native Californian, has three children, and traveled extensively while living abroad. A retired volunteer art docent, she started writing in her seventies and finds support from various writing groups. She's currently working on a novel based on her experiences after contracting polio as a child in the 1940s.

John T. Knox worked in the California public school system for more than 25 years, spending most of his time as a middle school science teacher. He co-founded an innovative back-to-nature program, emphasizing ecosystems, interdependence, and how nature works. He believes adults have a moral duty to leave behind a healthy, habitable planet to their children and fellow beings. In his view, no issue is more vital than addressing climate change. His current mission is to work as an advocate/activist for clean energy and sustainability. An avid hiker, birder, guitar player, and traveler, his writings appear in San Diego area newspapers.

Marissa C. Knox, Ph.D. is a writer, teacher, and researcher focused on cultivating holistic and collective well-being through mindfulness, compassion, and connection to nature. Marissa teaches college courses to help students cultivate healthy relationships and resilience, and she enjoys participating in creative journaling classes. She is the author of *g.r.a.c.e. and possibility*, a book of poetry, contemplations, and self-reflective writing practices to support living with integrity. In her teaching and writing, she guides others to embody their values, remember their interconnected wholeness, and connect to the miracle, mystery, and magic available in every moment.

Kimberly Krantz is the author of *Write Now. If I can create poetry, so can you!* - a book of her poems and a guide for writing poetry. Kim is an avid community volunteer, primarily through Epsilon Sigma Alpha, an international service organization. Her writing has won state and international-level awards in ESA's annual arts and literature competitions. She also teaches poetry writing and creativity. A native Californian, she grew up near the beach in Santa Monica, receiving writing inspiration from all forms of water. She and her husband reside in Orange County with their rescue dogs.

JG McCrillis a Midwest émigré to California, writes stories and poetry in San Juan Capistrano, CA. He has been published in a handful of small literary magazines, anthologies, and journals, including *Interstices: An Anthology*, Windflower Press (2010), *K*, Ontario, Canada (1990), *In Transit: Poetry for People on the Move*, Border Town Press (2014), *The Fiction Review* (1989).

Carol Ann Merker sold her first story in 1970 to Dick Van Dyke for his award-winning book *Faith, Hope, and Hilarity*. She was a first-page editor and writer for her high school newspaper, leading to her enjoyment of creative headlines. A certified scuba diver for many years, Carol journaled accounts of over 700 dives throughout the world. She now writes short stories about her travel and diving experiences and short memoirs about family events. Carol has actively participated in the Sea Country Journaling Workshop since 2016.

Laura Miller wrote her first poem as an eighth grade homework assignment and has never stopped writing poetry. A founding member of Wranch Writers in Claremont, she's been associated with Sea Country writers in Laguna Niguel for over a decade. Her publications include *Chopping Wood/ Carrying Water: a book of poems* (2017), *I've Seen the Mountains on the Moon* (2022), and *Lessons from Trails End* to be released in 2024. Her work has appeared in *The Sun Magazine, Art Journaling, San Clemente Magazine, San Clemente Life,* and Inland Empire publications. She also facilitates poetry workshops at Casa Romantica Cultural Center in San Clemente, CA.

Lee Milton has been writing most of his life and has heard many times, "Let me know when you write that book; I wanna read it." In college, he found the right major, Journalism, but rather than follow his passion, he joined the corporate world of sales/marketing and slogged through some wrong-headed jobs that paid the bills but didn't satisfy his talents. Much later in life, he decided to take writing seriously, joined some critique groups, and began his journey. He has recently finished his first generational novel and wonders if it'll ever see the printed page.

Nola Neeley is the author of *Flowers of the Heart, Growing Through Grief,* and finds inspiration in her weekly journal writing workshop in Laguna Niguel. After suffering the tragic loss of her eldest son, she discovered solace in writing, new friends, and a family more united. She's actively involved in her church community, reads at open mic events at Sea Country Center, and is working on another collection of poetry.

Gordon Nicholson taught science at Riverside Community College for 22 years while owning a landscaping business. His nature observations have been published weekly in a local newspaper. After retirement, he moved to Orange County, where he pursued his writing passion in journaling workshops facilitated by MaryAnn Easley. He enjoys writing in prose and poetic forms and looks forward to publishing further writings on nature.

Chris Perry learned to listen to the world and the things in it while growing up in Southern California. Now residing in Berkeley, he often spends his days wandering the streets, observing the scene, and listening to others. An avid reader, he eventually took an interest in writing poetry, documenting personal experiences about living in a complicated world. His current work in progress, *rose tree*, is a collection of poetry resulting from taking the road less traveled.

John Perry a poet born in Alaska and raised in small towns across the US, moved to Orange County in 2006 and frequently reads his poetry at open mic venues. His poems have been published in *Interstices An Anthology; Don't Blame the Ugly Mug* (Tebot Bach); and *Hummingbird Review*. His books of poetry include *Notes on Napkins* and *Where Do Butterflies Go When It Rains?* He's currently working on a book of San Francisco Bay area poems, comprised of both new and previously published poems. An incurable romantic, he actively participates in literary circles where he writes of love and loss, beaches, and San Francisco.

Nancy Pfaffl has enjoyed writing since childhood when she placed third in an essay contest, winning a briefcase for herself and a set of encyclopedias for her school. She's a member of the Sea Country journaling community and writes on numerous topics: memoir, current events, and poetry. Her 'found' poem, *Every Mother is Afraid*, pays homage to the women of Ukraine who protect their children while waiting for the return of husbands, sons, and brothers. A California resident since the age of one, she seeks inspiration from hiking, camping, and life near the seaside town of Dana Point.

Deborah Porter enjoys journaling and writing drabbles and short stories. Her current work-in-progress is a new-age romance novel, *Life Keeps Getting in My Way*. As a sales and cable TV executive, she wrote advertising and marketing campaigns, programming materials, and scripts. Her love of writing keeps her active in the community where she attends local writing classes and workshops.

Ghaffar Pourazar born to Iranian Azeri parents and British educated, gave up life as a computer animator to enroll in a Beijing opera school. Drawn by the difficulty of mastering the art form, he won the Golden Dragon Award and became known as the "Western Monkey King." The only Westerner to train in the art, he subsequently created the first bilingual version of the Monkey King opera. He also adapted Shakespeare's *A Midsummer Night's Dream* for the Beijing opera stage. He's currently in the US, appearing in stage productions and enjoying improv as he completes the writing of his long-awaited memoir.

Paula Shaffer Robertson is the author of *The Absent Mother: Memoir of a Foster Child* under the pen name Paula Shaffer. She's actively involved in a Laguna Niguel journaling class, contributes poetry at weekly read-aloud sessions, and reads at annual poetry events. She also writes book reviews for Story Circle Network, occasionally winning "Review of the Month." Poetry is the author's primary love, which she views as a source of soul healing. Her goal is to conduct poetry workshops with at-risk girls or incarcerated women.

Sheila Roell writes memoirs, poetry, travel, and other creative nonfiction stories. Her writing recently appeared in the 2022 anthology *Six Feet Apart – In the Time of Corona*. Her short stories have also been published in the Laguna Niguel Senior newsletter. As a former HR professional and technical writer, she enjoys writing competitions and the writing process, including beta reading, editing, and critique. Sheila is an active member of various writing groups, locally and nationally. She and her husband reside in Southern California.

Prem Saint is a Professor Emeritus of Geological Sciences at California State University, Fullerton. As a professor, he published scientific reports dealing with groundwater pollution, wetlands, and paleohydrology. For the past several years, Prem has been writing his memoir about his childhood in India, schooling in Kenya, university education in England and Minnesota, and professional work in Kenya and California. He credits MaryAnn Easley and her memoir and critique classes for his progress. He lives with his family in Southern California.

Jade Marie Smith is an award-winning author, poet, and photographer. An advocate for human rights, she encourages self-esteem and always brings light to difficult situations. Jade focuses on self-acceptance, growing from trauma, and breaking down walls. She's not afraid to put her personal hardships into her work to connect with others. She finishes her work with the words "PS. I Love You" to show her readers they are loved and cared for.

Olivia Starace lived for many years in Central America, becoming fluent in Spanish. Her poems have been published in college promotional materials and the quarterly *Desert Call*. Sensitive, lighthearted, and observant, she incorporates life events into her stories and poems. Olivia has translated her poems into interpretive dance, performing for church audiences. She receives her inspiration from writing groups across Orange County and enjoys sharing poetry with her fellow writers and at public events. She's a wife, mother, and grandmother, living with her husband, Vince, in Aliso Viejo, CA.

Setsuko Takemura is an artist with her main concentration in painting and ceramics. She has exhibited her work in Japan and the United States. She studied in Japan after graduating from Otis Art Institute with an MFA. While living in Kyoto, she began writing about her experiences. Semi-retired from a teaching career, she teaches art to children. Every year, she incorporates a poem with her New Year card drawing. She lives in Pasadena, California, and enjoys traveling with her husband.

Angela Tippell is the author of *Marietta's View, Stories from Westbourne Terrace Road*, and was born and raised in London. Her varied careers include working in the film industry, a boutique store, as a trade show model, and three decades as a trade show florist. This inspired her to start writing a memoir, *Jacqueline of all Trades, Mistress of None*. Although she has lived in California for more than half her life, the stories she writes most frequently occur in England. Her writing has been encouraged by her writing circle and critique group.

Mark Van Houten earned a doctorate in experimental neuroscience and published two dozen research manuscripts in journals as prestigious as science and nature magazines. After medical school at McGill University and a neurology residency at UCLA, he spent the next 35 years in clinical practice. In retirement, he enjoys writing music and short fiction; he will publish his first collection of short stories in 2023.

Sharon Voorhees was born in southern Indiana, has been writing since high school and journaling daily most of her life. After moving to California at 24, she took several creative writing, journalism, and media classes at Saddleback College in South Orange County, CA. In the early 2000s, she'd acquired the skills to start her own proofreading/editing business. In recent years, she has taken memoir and poetry classes and is actively involved in an advanced writer's critique group. Sharon writes from the heart, creating beautiful images and metaphors. To her, writing is like breathing, a joyful part of her life.

Karen Ward is an erstwhile lawyer and family eulogist. She writes poetry and memoir as she mines her life for meaning. Her writing has appeared in the anthologies *Baja Benediction* and *No Mi Olivide,* and *The Vassar Quarterly*. She enjoys sharing writing and the process of critique with fellow writers in Orange County, California.

MJ West is the author of *No Reservations*, a memoir, and *A Little Bit of This and a Little Bit of That,* a collection of recipes handed down from her Italian family. She received awards in 2018 and 2019 in the Laguna Beach Poetry Contest for *Irish Farewell* and *Interlude.* She has also been published in quarterly journals of the California State Poetry Society. Her reflections on life experiences have been published in journals and anthologies of Story Circle Network, a national organization for women memoir writers. She resides with her husband of sixty-four years in San Clemente, California.

NOTE: To contact any author in the Writers Collective regarding their marketing materials, press releases, or information about individual books, upcoming appearances, events, or speaking engagements, call/text the publisher at Windflower Press: 949-285-3831. To order additional copies of this book, visit amazon.com.

Acknowledgments

As curators of this book, we worked with a talented group of thirty-nine authors. We want to thank and acknowledge each writer for contributing a piece of their heart and soul, sharing the intricacies of family life, and allowing the readers to experience or share a laugh about how they overcame challenges. Whether or not we sit in a classroom together, connect across the country via the internet, or wait to meet for the first time, it is apparent that all authors in this collection share a passion for writing. Decades of life experiences, told through eighty-six poems and stories, proves that as we may write alone, we remain part of a thoughtful and dedicated community.

Thank you to Jann Harmon, our graphic designer. The ability to transform a few words into a cover plus layout poems and stories with artistic flair is a unique skill you use so well.

Thank you to Yvonne Davis, our beta reader for your generous contribution.

Thank you, readers! We hope you enjoyed reading this book offered by The Writers Collective.

~ MaryAnn, Kim, & Sheila

"Writing and reading decrease our sense of isolation. They deepen and widen and expand our sense of life: they feed the soul. When writers make us shake our heads with the exactness of their prose and their truths, and even make us laugh about ourselves or life, our buoyancy is restored. We are given a shot at dancing with, or at least clapping along with, the absurdity of life, instead of being squashed by it over and over again. It's like singing on a boat during a terrible storm at sea. You can't stop the raging storm, but singing can change the hearts and spirits of the people who are together on that ship."

—Anne Lamott, *Bird by Bird*